Thyme for Dessert

Thyme for Dessert

Sweets and Treats Inspired by the Flavours of the Pacific Northwest Coast

DL ACKEN
with **AURELIA LOUVET**

Foreword by Chef Heidi Fink

Copyright © 2025 by DL Acken
Photographs copyright © 2025 by DL Acken

All rights reserved. No part of this publication may be reproduced, stored in a retrieval system, or transmitted in any form or by any means, electronic, mechanical, photocopying, recording, or otherwise, without the prior written permission of the publisher. For more information, contact the publisher at:

TouchWood Editions
Touchwoodeditions.com

The information in this book is true and complete to the best of the author's knowledge. All recommendations are made without guarantee on the part of the author or the publisher.

Recipe contributions by Aurelia Louvet
Edited by Lesley Cameron
Copy edited by Christine Savage
Proofread by Meg Yamamoto
Index by Janice Logan
Cover and interior design by Jazmin Welch

CATALOGUING DATA AVAILABLE FROM LIBRARY AND ARCHIVES CANADA

ISBN 9781771514804 (hardcover)
ISBN 9781771514811 (electronic)

TouchWood Editions gratefully acknowledges that the land on which we live and work is within the traditional territories of the Lkwungen (Esquimalt and Songhees), Malahat, Pacheedaht, Scia'new, T'Sou-ke, and W̱SÁNEĆ (Pauquachin, Tsartlip, Tsawout, and Tseycum) peoples.

We acknowledge the financial support of the Government of Canada through the Canada Book Fund, and the province of British Columbia through the Book Publishing Tax Credit.

This book was produced using FSC®-certified, acid-free papers, processed chlorine free, and printed with soya-based inks.

Printed in China

29 28 27 26 25   1 2 3 4 5

For Aurelia,
with whom everything in life is sweeter

and for Lesley,
who taught me to cook and encouraged
me every step of the way

FOREWORD *ix*

Introduction *1*

Confections & Cookies *3*

Breads & Bars *39*

Cakes, Cobblers & Crumbles *67*

Pies & Pastries *99*

Ice Creams & Custards *133*

Preserving *159*

ACKNOWLEDGEMENTS *166*

INDEX *167*

FOREWORD

Thyme for Dessert is a cookbook that reflects what it feels like to live here on the West Coast. As I flip through these pages, seeing the beautiful photographs and inspired recipes, I am transported instantly to a kitchen with a view of the trees and the water, a kitchen filled with the wonderful aroma of home baking.

If anyone can be trusted to present us with a definitive Pacific coast cookbook, it is Danielle Acken. She makes her home on beautiful Salt Spring Island, a jewel of the Salish Sea. She co-authored and photographed the award-winning *Cedar + Salt: Vancouver Island Recipes from Forest, Farm, Field, and Sea,* and her food photography business is internationally acclaimed. I am lucky to count her as a colleague in the food scene here on the islands.

Her new book, *Thyme for Dessert,* is beautiful, homey, and inspiring. I instantly want to make every recipe in it! The recipe titles alone have me tasting the flavours and textures as if I had the baked items in front of me. The McClintock Buffalo Milk Cheesecake gets an instant bookmark; I keenly anticipate the rich creamy tang of that first bite. And that Spruce Tip Shortbread . . . I can already taste the indefinable floral resin of spruce tips, and feel the sweet sandy crumble as the flavours dissolve in my mouth.

With every page and every recipe, I am inspired and excited. With its inventive combinations (Ginger, Pear & Parsnip Cake, anyone?), with its homage to tradition while still giving us an exciting local twist (see: Herb-Scented Marshmallows with Nootka rose), this is the kind of cookbook I dream about.

I am brought to the forest, to the garden, to the sea, to my home. The extensive use of indigenous ingredients throughout this cookbook reminds me to thank the Coast Salish, Nuu-chah-nulth, and Kwakwaka'wakw peoples who are long-time stewards of these lands and their treasures. The nod to Danielle's personal heritage, as well as to the influences of all the cultures who touch the Pacific, adds richness and flexibility to the host of wonderful recipes and flavour combinations in this book. And every chapter opens with a chef-approved list of tips for success in your baking endeavours.

Thyme for Dessert is part culinary handbook, part love letter to our home. The evocative images and tantalizing recipes pay homage to this magical place. Whether you live here, once visited, or dream of visiting, this cookbook will bring you a sense of being here on the Pacific, and bring both comfort and adventure to your kitchen.

—CHEF HEIDI FINK

Introduction

THE RECIPES IN THIS BOOK are inspired by the abundance of flavours that surrounded me when I was growing up on Canada's western islands. From the glut of wild indigenous ingredients that flourish on the lands of the Coast Salish, Nuu-chah-nulth, and Kwakwaka'wakw peoples to the myriad of international influences delivered through layers of both Asian and European culinary traditions, the combinations of available ingredients offer a distinctly West Coast twist to many of my favourite traditional baked goods and desserts. In this book, shortbread finds new glam with the addition of spruce tips, cannoli cones get a hit of umami from the inclusion of shiro miso paste, and fruit-filled soda bread transforms into biscotti-style crackers to adorn the classic after-dinner cheese plate.

While these recipes may sound hyper-local, they're also readily accessible to the home baker. Each dish in this book has an easily replicated traditional base enhanced by the addition of coastal ingredients and flavours, most of which can be switched out for whatever you have on hand. Don't have fresh fruit? No worries: in most cases a good quality frozen version will do. Can't find a local varietal such as haskaps or sour cherries? Swap them out respectively for blackberries and sweet Bing or Rainier cherries. And if you don't have a garden overflowing with fresh produce and herbs, most grocery stores carry local fruits in the summer and fresh herbs all year round. At the back of the book, you'll find tips and tricks for preserving these ingredients so that you can create the recipes whenever you want.

This collection is meant to inspire, to show how a twist on tradition can lead to something new and innovative. Feel free to experiment, to integrate your own favourite flavour combinations into the base recipe to create something all your own. Whether your end-of-meal tastes lean toward lemony tartness, salty caramel, deep and delicious chocolate, or a traditional cheese plate, I hope this book holds at least one dish that becomes a firm favourite for years to come.

Confections & Cookies

Spruce Tip Shortbread *11*

Sesame-Laced Miso Biscuits *15*

Miso Cannoli with Lemony Chèvre Crème *18*

Herb-Scented Marshmallows *22*

Sea Salted Caramel Apples *25*

Whiskey-Spiked Tamari Bear Claws *28*

Truffles of the Forest *31*
Dark Chocolate Spruce *34*
Milk Chocolate Mint *35*
White Chocolate Rose *36*
Swirled-Chocolate Lemon Balm *37*

COOKIES ARE OFTEN THE FIRST DESSERTS that people experiment with, and for good reason! They're easy to whip up and they can please a crowd easily. Although cookie recipes are generally not overly complex, I've listed a few tips and tricks to ensure you get a great bake every time.

In contrast, making your own candies and confections may sound intimidating, but a good set of tools and some basic instructions will help get you on your way. Candy-making often involves working with sugar and chocolate, and it can be a bit like conducting a science experiment: follow the step-by-step directions and your end results should be consistent each and every time. I've listed a few tips below to increase your chances of success when you're working with these ingredients.

- Be sure that your eggs and butter are at the correct temperature. Some recipes require room-temperature butter, and some require refrigerator-cold or even frozen. Temperature is often key to how the butter and sugar come together as well as how cookies spread while they're in the oven. Cold eggs will seize room-temperature butter, so be sure to take them out of the refrigerator to come to room temperature before you begin baking.
- When you cream sugar and butter, beat them on high speed until they start to change colour. You're not just mixing the sugar and butter together; you're introducing air and changing the molecular structure to create something new. The butter should become a lighter yellow colour and lightly whipped and fluffy.
- If the recipe specifies how far apart to place cookie dough balls on the tray, do what it tells you. Some cookies spread a lot, and you don't want them to meld into each other.
- Chill cookie dough balls for 10 minutes in the refrigerator before baking. For cookies such as chocolate chip and oatmeal raisin, this will slow their spread by melting the butter more slowly, giving them a nice, even shape and preventing you from having thin cookies that have all baked into each other.
- Dark, black, and older baking trays will bake cookies faster than newer, light grey ones, so be sure to watch your time depending on the colour of your trays.
- Bake cookies on the centre rack of the oven (unless instructed to do otherwise). You want even heat around them so that they all cook at the same rate. If you're baking multiple trays of cookies at the same time, be sure to rotate their position midway through baking so that they are all finished at the same time.
- If you're baking on parchment paper, slide the cookies on the paper onto a cooling rack as soon as you can when they come out of the oven unless the instructions specifically say to let them cool for a period on the tray. This stops them from continuing to bake for a few minutes on a hot tray, even when it's sitting on a cooling rack.
- If you're making candy, invest in a good quality candy thermometer and read the instructions before you use it. Sugar is an interesting and volatile ingredient, and it reacts differently depending on what temperature it's heated to. Do not touch hot sugar—and don't even think about tasting it. It becomes molten hot quickly as it cooks and will cause severe burns. Be sure to cool any sugar confections as directed in the recipes.

- Following the recipe instructions and using the candy thermometer makes candy-making safe and easy. Sugar reacts differently at each temperature level, so you'll need to keep a close eye on the thermometer to ensure that you reach the cooking stage needed to achieve your desired consistency once the sugar cools.
- Do not add water to hot sugar. It will seize, turning into a hard lump of white crystallized sugar, and you'll have to start again.
- Chocolate on direct heat will burn in a matter of moments. Always melt chocolate in a double boiler. If you melt it in the microwave, check it every 20 seconds or so.
- Any water, even steam droplets from water boiling in a double boiler, will seize melted chocolate instantly. Be sure that all tools that come in contact with warm chocolate are clean and dry.
- Tempering chocolate means manipulating the fat molecules in the cocoa butter to achieve that classic beautifully glossy appearance, smooth texture, and satisfying snap when you bite into it. Untempered chocolate looks dull and feels chalky in your mouth.
- When tempering chocolate, the 50-50 rule works well. Melt half of your chopped chocolate in the top of a double boiler set over water until your candy thermometer shows 115°F (46°C) for bittersweet or semisweet chocolate and 110°F (43°C) for milk and white chocolate. Remove the top of the double boiler from the heat, add the remaining chopped chocolate, and continue to stir until the thermometer shows between 84°F (29°C) and 89°F (31.5°C).
- 89°F (31.5°C) is the ideal working temperature for tempered chocolate. If you find that your already tempered chocolate starts to get too solid to dip into, you can reheat it to that temperature in the double boiler and then continue working.
- Tempered chocolate will stay crisp and hard at room temperature.

Spruce Tip Shortbread

MAKES 24 COOKIES + 1 CUP (250 ML) SYRUP

Spruce tips are a quintessential West Coast ingredient, and one that is often used in cocktails but overlooked when it comes to desserts. Here the buttery shortbread complements the earthy sweet scent of the sugared spruce. This recipe takes some planning because you prepare the spruce tip syrup two weeks ahead of time, but it's so worth it! (And the syrup will keep for a couple of months in the refrigerator.) The shortbread can be made without the spruce and is also delicious with toasted, crushed hazelnuts or lavender buds. Make the dough in advance and keep it in the refrigerator for up to a week to slice and bake fresh cookies as desired.

SPRUCE TIP SYRUP

1 cup (250 mL) packed dark brown sugar
1 cup (250 mL) freshly picked green spruce tips

SHORTBREAD

¾ cup (180 mL) unsalted butter, room temperature
¼ cup (60 mL) granulated sugar
2–3 wet spruce tips from the spruce tip syrup
½ cup (125 mL) packed dark brown sugar
½ tsp (2.5 mL) fine sea salt
2¼ cup (560 mL) all-purpose flour
⅓ cup (80 mL) whole milk
1 cup (250 mL) icing sugar
2 Tbsp (30 mL) spruce tip syrup
2 Tbsp (30 mL) lemon juice

SPRUCE TIP SYRUP

1. In a 2-cup (500 mL) mason jar, layer the brown sugar and spruce tips. Start with the sugar, then lay down a few tips, cover with sugar, lay down some more tips, and repeat until you've used all the ingredients. Secure the lid tightly and place the jar in a window where sunlight can reach it. The UV rays will break down the tips and begin the fermenting process.
2. Every day for 2 weeks, flip the jar over so that it's on its lid one day, its bottom the next. After 2 weeks, a dark, sugary, fragrant syrup should have formed.
3. This will keep for 2–3 months in the refrigerator. (The tips can be stored for 1 month.)

SHORTBREAD

1. Cut the butter into 1-inch (2.5 cm) cubes and place them in a large, flat-bottomed skillet over medium heat. Let the butter melt, moving it around constantly with a wooden spoon. Once fully melted, the butter will begin to foam and sizzle. Continue to cook, stirring constantly, until the butter turns a deep golden colour and the milk solids at the bottom of the pan are a toasty brown, 3–5 minutes. Remove from the heat and set aside to cool to room temperature. Transfer the cooled brown butter into a 1-cup (250 mL) wide-mouth mason jar fitted with a lid and place in the refrigerator to solidify.

>

2 While the butter is chilling, place the granulated sugar and the 2–3 wet spruce tips from the syrup in a mortar and grind with a pestle until the sugar is completely infused with the spruce. If you don't have a mortar and pestle, you can use a food processor or even a kitchen knife to finely chop the spruce and then use your fingers to rub the spruce into the sugar.

3 Take the solid browned butter out of the refrigerator and place it in a large bowl or the bowl of a stand mixer fitted with a paddle attachment. Add the spruce sugar and the brown sugar. Beat on medium-high speed until well mixed and fluffy. Add the sea salt and then gradually add the flour, about ½ cup (125 mL) at a time, mixing on low speed, then add the milk to form a soft dough.

4 Remove the dough from the mixing bowl and use your hands to form a log of 10 inches (25 cm) by 2 inches (5 cm). Wrap the log tightly in plastic wrap and place in the refrigerator for at least 2 hours.

5 Preheat the oven to 350°F (175°C). Line two baking sheets with parchment paper.

6 Unwrap the cookie dough and use a knife to cut 24 cookie discs of ½-inch (1.25 cm) thickness. Place the cookies on the prepared pans at least 2 inches (5 cm) apart.

7 Bake the cookies until they are firm and just slightly golden around the edges, 15–20 minutes. Let sit for 3–4 minutes on the pan after removing from the oven, then transfer the cookies and the parchment paper to cooling racks and let them cool completely.

8 Mix the icing sugar with the spruce tip syrup and the lemon juice and stir until completely combined. Drizzle or dip the cooled cookies as desired and place on a cooling rack until the glaze has dried.

9 Cookies will last for up to 10 days in an airtight container, or 3 months in the freezer.

NOTE: The syrup is delicious in cocktails that use a simple syrup. The tips can be stored in their syrup in the refrigerator for up to 1 month and used in place of mint, rosemary, or thyme in various recipes such as Chocolate, Cherry & Lemon Thyme Bread Pudding (page 53), Apple Cheddar Rosemary Pie (page 113), or Italian Plum & Thyme Crumble (page 89). It also makes an incredible addition along with caramel to the base Vanilla Bean Ice Cream recipe (page 143).

Sesame-Laced Miso Biscuits

MAKES APPROXIMATELY 30 COOKIES

This twist on the classic French lace biscuit layers in umami-packed Asian flavours and provides a satisfyingly sweet crunch. These elevated cookies are great for everyday tea times and also make a wonderful addition to any special-occasion dessert tray.

- ½ cup (125 mL) unsalted butter, room temperature, cubed
- ¾ cup (180 mL) almond flour
- ⅔ cup (160 mL) packed dark brown sugar
- 3 Tbsp (45 mL) sesame seeds
- 1 Tbsp (15 mL) golden or dark corn syrup
- 2 tsp (10 mL) shiro miso (white) paste
- 1 cup (250 mL) finely chopped semisweet chocolate

1. In a medium saucepan set over medium heat, melt the butter and then add the flour, sugar, sesame seeds, syrup, and miso. Whisk vigorously until the ingredients are well combined, 1–2 minutes. Remove the pot from the heat and let the mixture sit for 10 minutes. It will thicken as it cools.
2. Preheat the oven to 350°F (175°C). Line two or three large baking sheets with parchment paper or silicone baking mats.
3. Place heaping teaspoon measures of cookie dough 3 inches (7.5 cm) apart on the prepared baking sheets. Bake each tray separately until the cookies are golden brown around the edges, 6–8 minutes.
4. Remove the cookies from the oven and allow them to cool and begin to set for 10 minutes on the baking sheets before transferring them directly to cooling racks to cool and crisp completely.
5. When the cookies are completely cooled, line the baking sheets with fresh sheets of parchment paper.
6. Heat ½ cup (125 mL) of the chocolate in a double boiler over medium heat until melted. Remove from the heat and add the remaining chocolate. Whisk until all the chocolate is melted. Let sit for 2 minutes and then, one by one, dip the cookies halfway into the chocolate. Shake off the excess chocolate and place the cookies on the parchment paper to let the chocolate firm up.
7. Once the chocolate has set, the cookies can be stored in an airtight container in the refrigerator for up to 7 days or in the freezer for up to 3 months.

Miso Cannoli with Lemony Chèvre Crème

MAKES 12 CANNOLI

Traditional Italian cannoli get a delicious makeover with the addition of sweet and salty shiro miso and the lemony sweet tartness of Salt Spring Island goat cheese filling. You'll need cannoli tubes for this recipe: they are hollow metal forms that you wrap the cannoli dough around to set the shape while frying. They cool quickly and allow the cannoli to slide off easily. You can find them at most kitchen stores or online.

2 Tbsp (30 mL) apple cider vinegar
1 Tbsp (15 mL) shiro miso (white) paste
1½ cups (375 mL) all-purpose flour, plus more for rolling
2 Tbsp (30 mL) granulated sugar
½ tsp (2.5 mL) fine sea salt
3 Tbsp (45 mL) unsalted butter, cold, cubed
1 large egg, cold

1½ cups (375 mL) soft chèvre, such as fresh goat cheese from Salt Spring Island Cheese
¾ cups (180 mL) icing sugar, plus more for dusting
1 Tbsp (15 mL) grated lemon zest
1 Tbsp (15 mL) lemon juice
1 egg white
Canola oil for frying; enough for 3 inches (7.5 cm) deep in a wide, heavy-bottomed pot

1. In a small bowl, whisk together the apple cider vinegar and miso to make a paste. Set aside.
2. In the bowl of a food processor fitted with a steel blade, combine the flour, sugar, and sea salt. Add the butter and pulse until the mixture resembles small pebbles. Add the egg and the apple cider vinegar miso paste and pulse again, just until the dough begins to hold together. Transfer the dough to a floured surface and knead by hand until smooth, 3–4 minutes. Wrap in plastic wrap and refrigerate for at least 1 hour, or up to overnight.
3. Using a stand mixer fitted with a whisk attachment (or a large mixing bowl and a handheld electric mixer), whisk the chèvre, icing sugar, lemon zest, and lemon juice on high speed until light and fluffy, about 1 minute. Cover the bowl with plastic or beeswax wrap and set in the refrigerator until needed.
4. Divide the dough into 12 evenly sized balls. Lightly coat a rolling pin and the countertop with flour and roll the balls out to no more than ⅛-inch (0.3 cm) thickness. If you have one, a tortilla press works really well to form the thin pastry circles quickly and easily.
5. Place the egg white in a small bowl, whisk until frothy, and set aside.
6. In a wide, heavy-bottomed pot fitted with a thermometer, heat the canola oil to between 350°F (175°C) and 380°F (193°C). Line a large plate with paper towels.
7. Wrap one circle of dough loosely around a cannoli tube. Brush one end of the dough with egg white, then pull the other end over the top and press down firmly to seal. Repeat with three more shells.

8 Use tongs to carefully lower the cannoli forms into the oil and, turning them often, fry until golden, 2–3 minutes. Remove the shells from the oil with the tongs and transfer them to the prepared plate to cool. Once the shells are cool, carefully remove the forms and repeat until all 12 cannoli are done. Cool completely before filling.

9 Remove the filling from the refrigerator 30 minutes before you're ready to fill the cannoli. Give the mixture a whisk and then load a piping bag fitted with a 1-inch (2.5 cm) nozzle with the lemony chèvre filling. Insert the tip into one end of a shell and pipe the cream in, filling it halfway, and then pipe the rest in the other end. Repeat with the remaining shells. Dust the filled cannoli with icing sugar and serve immediately.

10 The shells and filling can be stored separately for up to 3 days. Store the shells in an airtight container at room temperature and the filling in an airtight container in the refrigerator. Filled cannoli can be frozen in an airtight container for up to 3 months. Thaw for at least 2 hours before serving.

Herb-Scented Marshmallows

MAKES APPROXIMATELY 24 LARGE MARSHMALLOWS

If you haven't tried marshmallows scented with garden-grown herbs before, you're in for a treat! The essence of lavender or rosemary marshmallows in a hot cup of cocoa or toasted over a campfire brings a whole new level of deliciousness to this classic confection. If you're feeling experimental, try mixing things up with some of your own favourite herbs and wild flavours: Nootka rose, spruce, and lemon balm all work well. Simply swap the herbs out in a 1-to-1 ratio. Marshmallows have a 6-hour cure time, so be prepared to make them in advance.

1 cup (250 mL) water, divided
3 packets (each 7 g) Knox unflavoured gelatin
2 cups (500 mL) granulated sugar
½ cup (125 mL) agave syrup
Pinch of fine sea salt
1 cup (250 mL) icing sugar, divided
½ cup (125 mL) cornstarch

FOR LAVENDER

1–2 drops lavender culinary oil (I love the oil from Lavender & Black)
1 Tbsp (15 mL) culinary lavender buds, ground to dust in a coffee grinder

FOR ROSEMARY

1–2 drops rosemary culinary oil
1 Tbsp (15 mL) finely chopped fresh rosemary, ground to dust in a coffee grinder

1 Lightly grease a 9- × 13-inch (23 × 33 cm) glass baking dish with shortening, coconut oil, or butter.
2 Pour ½ cup (125 mL) of the water into the bowl of a stand mixer fitted with a paddle attachment (or a large mixing bowl). Sprinkle the gelatin over the top of the water, stir gently, and set aside to dissolve.
3 In a small saucepan, combine the sugar, agave syrup, sea salt, and remaining ½ cup (125 mL) of water. Place over medium heat and stir gently with a wooden spoon until the sugar dissolves and the mixture comes to a boil. Place a candy thermometer on the side of the pot with the tip inserted into the syrup and continue boiling, without stirring, until the mixture reaches 240°F (116°C). Immediately remove from the heat.
4 Turn the mixer on to low speed and slowly pour the hot syrup into the gelatin. Once all the syrup has been added, gradually increase the speed to high. Beat until the mixture is very thick, 3–5 minutes. To check if the marshmallow mixture is ready, stop the mixer and dip a spoon into the bowl. If long ribbons form when you pull the spoon up, the marshmallow is almost done.
5 Add the lavender or rosemary oil. Beat on high speed for another 10–15 seconds to incorporate the oil, then immediately pour the mixture into the prepared baking dish. The marshmallow will be sticky, so wet your hands and a spatula to pack it into the baking dish more easily. Let sit for at least 6 hours.

6. When the marshmallow has cured, whisk together ¾ cup (180 mL) of the icing sugar with the cornstarch in a mixing bowl, then put it through a fine mesh sieve to ensure there are no clumps. In another small bowl, place the remaining icing sugar and either the ground lavender buds or the ground rosemary. Whisk together until clump-free.
7. Generously coat a large cutting board with approximately one-third of the icing sugar-cornstarch mixture and turn the set marshmallow out onto the dusted surface. Using a sieve, cover the top of the marshmallow brick with the remaining icing sugar-cornstarch mixture. Dust a large chef's knife with this mixture before cutting the marshmallows into 24 evenly sized pieces. Toss each marshmallow in the herbed sugar until thoroughly coated.
8. Store in a large, airtight container at room temperature for up to 1 month.

Sea Salted Caramel Apples

MAKES 8–10 CARAMEL APPLES

This is one of my most cherished childhood fairground favourites, taken to new heights with the addition of good quality West Coast rum—I like Merridale Cidery's Cowichan Spiced Rhumb—and artisanal island sea salts in a variety of flavours. If you're making these for the kids, you can replace the rum with the same volume of vanilla extract.

3 cups (750 mL) water, divided
8–10 firm, tart apples such as Granny Smith or Pink Lady, stems removed, skins on
1½ cups (375 mL) light brown sugar
1 cup (250 mL) light corn syrup
1¾ cup (430 mL) whipping cream
¼ cup (60 mL) unsalted butter
2 Tbsp (30 mL) good quality dark rum
8–10 apple sticks or chopsticks
2 Tbsp (30 mL) large crystal artisan sea salt (lemon and rosemary flavours work well; see page 163)

1 Place the water in a medium saucepan and bring to a boil over high heat. While the water boils, use a slotted spoon to carefully dip each of the apples in the water for approximately 30 seconds. Don't worry, this won't cook them. It will simply clean them and remove any residual wax, allowing the caramel to stick. Dry the apples thoroughly and chill until needed.
2 Line a baking sheet with a silicone mat.
3 In a medium-sized, heavy-bottomed saucepan, place the brown sugar, corn syrup, whipping cream, and butter. Place on the stove over medium heat and cook while stirring with a wooden spoon until the butter has melted. Place a candy thermometer on the side of the pot and continue to cook over medium heat until the thermometer reads 240°F (116°C). Stay close as the caramel will begin to bubble and froth at the halfway mark—don't turn down the temperature, just stir with a wooden spoon to settle it down.
4 Once the caramel reaches 240°F (116°C), remove the pot from the heat and stir in the rum. Let the caramel cool for about 5 minutes, stirring occasionally.
5 Meanwhile, insert the sticks into the apples. Dip an apple into the caramel three or four times, tilting it from side to side to cover it completely. Lift the apple out of the caramel and shake to remove any excess. Place the apple on the silicone mat and sprinkle immediately with sea salt. Repeat with the remaining apples.

NOTE: If the caramel begins to get too firm to dip the apples into, just place the pot back on the stove long enough to warm and soften it.

Whiskey-Spiked Tamari Bear Claws

MAKES 30–36 BEAR CLAWS

Not just for the holiday season, these classic chocolatey confections are easy enough to make whenever your sweet tooth calls for attention. The tamari almonds pack a salty punch that perfectly complements the sweet, whiskey-spiked, chewy caramel. My dearest friend, Aurelia Louvet, the queen of sweet things, gave me this recipe, which doubles and triples well, making it perfect for gift-giving.

2 cups (500 mL) raw almonds
2 Tbsp (30 mL) tamari
½ cup (125 mL) unsalted butter, cold, cubed
½ cup (125 mL) whipping cream
¼ cup (60 mL) golden syrup
3 Tbsp (45 mL) water
1 cup (250 mL) granulated sugar
2 Tbsp (30 mL) good quality whiskey
12 oz (340 g) semisweet or dark chocolate, finely chopped and divided
Flaky sea salt to finish

1. Preheat the oven to 300°F (150°C). Line a baking sheet with parchment paper.
2. In a medium bowl, toss the almonds with the tamari until well coated. Spread the almonds out on the prepared baking sheet in a single layer. Bake for 10 minutes. Remove the almonds from the oven, flip them over, and bake until they are dry and fragrant, approximately 8 minutes. Watch carefully so they don't burn. Remove from the oven and let cool on the pan.
3. In a small saucepan set over medium heat, melt the butter. Pour the cream into a small bowl or jug and add the melted butter. Set aside.
4. In a tall, medium-sized saucepan, mix the syrup with the water. Gently stir the sugar into the liquid until it's moist and then place the pot over medium heat. Attach a candy thermometer to the side of the saucepan and cook without stirring until the temperature reads 320°F (160°C) and the sugar is a light amber colour, 5–8 minutes.
5. Turn off the heat, remove the candy thermometer, and then slowly pour the butter and cream mixture into the sugar. The sugar will bubble and sputter, so be careful. Whisk the mixture quickly to incorporate the cream and butter. Don't worry if the sugar seizes. It will soften again as it boils. Turn the heat on to between medium and medium-low, return the candy thermometer to the pot, and continue cooking until the caramel reaches 240°F (116°C), another 5–8 minutes. Remove the pot from the heat, whisk in the whiskey, and set aside until the mixture begins to cool and thicken, 15–20 minutes.
6. Line a baking sheet with parchment paper.
7. Cluster four or five almonds together on the prepared tray. Using a small spoon, drizzle caramel over the centre of them. Repeat with the remaining almonds. Place the tray in the refrigerator to set the caramel.
8. Place a cooling rack over a parchment paper-lined baking sheet.

9 Gently melt 9 oz (255 g) of the chocolate in a double boiler over medium-low heat, stirring until it's fully melted. Remove from the heat and stir in the remaining chocolate. Stir until fully incorporated and melted. This will temper the chocolate and add a smooth finish to the candies.

10 Place the caramel-coated almond clusters on the prepared cooling rack and lightly spoon the warm chocolate over the centre, allowing the excess to drip onto the pan. Lightly sprinkle flaky sea salt over the candies.

11 Store in an airtight container at room temperature for up to 5 days, refrigerate for up to 3 weeks, or freeze for up to 3 months. Thaw frozen candies thoroughly before serving.

Truffles of the Forest

MAKES 24 TRUFFLES FOR EACH FLAVOUR

Dark Chocolate Spruce
Milk Chocolate Mint
White Chocolate Rose
Swirled Chocolate Lemon Balm

Truffles are the ultimate in chocolate decadence, and they're also one of the easiest candies to make at home. These truffles are creamy, delicious, and scented with flavours of the forest, and the hardest part of making them will be trying to choose a favourite from spruce, mint, rose, or lemon balm, all of which grow in wild abundance here on the islands.

Dark Chocolate Spruce

10 oz (285 g) dark or semisweet chocolate
½ cup (125 mL) whipping cream
2 Tbsp (30 mL) unsalted butter, room temperature
½ cup (125 mL) washed, dried, and roughly chopped fresh spruce tips, divided
½ cup (125 mL) granulated sugar

1. Finely chop the chocolate and place it in a medium-sized heatproof bowl. Set aside.
2. In a small saucepan, combine the cream, butter, and ¼ cup (60 mL) of the spruce tips. Heat on medium until just scalded. Small bubbles will appear along the edge but the cream should not reach a boil. Remove from the heat and let sit for 15 minutes to infuse. Reheat for 3–4 minutes to bring the temperature up, but do not allow to boil.
3. Remove the cream from the heat and pour it through a fine mesh strainer into the chocolate. Whisk until all the chocolate is melted. Let this truffle mixture cool at room temperature for 1 hour and then cover the bowl tightly and place in the refrigerator for another hour.
4. Line a baking tray with parchment paper.
5. Once the chocolate is chilled, use a small melon ball scooper to portion out 1-inch (2.5 cm) diameter balls of chocolate. Using your hands, roll the balls to even out their shape and place them on the prepared baking tray.
6. In a food processor fitted with a steel blade, pulse the remaining ¼ cup (60 mL) of spruce tips with the sugar until fully incorporated and a fine powder forms. Roll the truffles in this sugar mixture to coat.
7. Store in an airtight container in the refrigerator for up to 2 weeks.

Milk Chocolate Mint

10 oz (285 g) milk chocolate
½ cup (125 mL) whipping cream
2 Tbsp (30 mL) unsalted butter
3–4 sprigs mint, washed, dried, and roughly chopped (chocolate mint, spearmint, or peppermint)
¼ cup (60 mL) Dutch processed cocoa powder

1. Follow steps 1–5 of the dark chocolate spruce recipe, replacing the dark chocolate with milk chocolate and adding the mint instead of the spruce tips in step 2.
2. Roll the truffles in the cocoa powder to coat.
3. Store in an airtight container in the refrigerator for up to 2 weeks.

White Chocolate Rose

14 oz (400 g) pure white chocolate, finely chopped, divided
½ cup (125 mL) whipping cream
2 Tbsp (30 mL) unsalted butter
¼ cup (60 mL) rose petals, preferably wild Nootka, bruised with the back of a knife
Dried rose petals or rosebuds

1 Place 10 oz (285 g) of the chopped white chocolate in a medium-sized heatproof bowl. Set aside.
2 Follow steps 2–5 of the dark chocolate spruce recipe, adding the bruised rose petals instead of the spruce tips in step 2.
3 Place 2 oz (56 g) of the remaining white chocolate in a double boiler over medium heat and stir until fully melted and a candy thermometer reads 110°F (43°C). Remove the pot from the heat, add the remaining 2 oz (56 g) of chocolate, and continue to stir until fully melted and the thermometer reads 85°F (29°C). Pour into a tall glass.
4 Line a baking sheet with parchment paper.
5 Using a long skewer, spear the truffle balls one at a time, dip them into the melted chocolate, shake off the excess, and place them on the parchment paper. Sprinkle with dried rose petals and let the chocolate dry at room temperature.
6 Store in an airtight container in the refrigerator for up to 2 weeks.

Swirled-Chocolate Lemon Balm

5 oz (142 g) dark bitter chocolate, finely chopped
5 oz (142 g) white chocolate, finely chopped
½ cup (125 mL) whipping cream
2 Tbsp (30 mL) unsalted butter
5–6 sprigs lemon balm, washed and thoroughly dried
1 cup (250 mL) freeze-dried raspberries or strawberries

1. Place the finely chopped dark chocolate in a small mixing bowl, and the white chocolate in another. Set the bowls aside.
2. Follow step 2 of the dark chocolate spruce recipe, adding the lemon balm instead of the spruce tips.
3. Remove the lemon balm sprigs. Pour half of the warmed cream into each bowl of chocolate and stir well to combine. Let cool at room temperature for 1 hour. Combine the two chocolate ganaches in a shallow bowl and, using a skewer, gently swirl them together. Cover the bowl tightly and place in the refrigerator for another hour.
4. Follow steps 4–5 of the dark chocolate spruce recipe.
5. Pulse the freeze-dried berries in a food processor fitted with a steel blade until only a fine powder remains. Roll the truffles in the powder to coat.
6. Store in an airtight container in the refrigerator for up to 2 weeks.

Breads & Bars

Masala Chai Spiced Buttermilk Doughnuts *46*

Apple Rosemary Fritters *49*

Apple & Aged-Cheddar Scones *51*

Chocolate, Cherry & Lemon Thyme Bread Pudding with Red Wine Reduction *53*

Chocolate Walnut Zucchini Bread *59*

Dried-Fruit Soda Bread Biscotti *61*

Toasted Hazelnut Chocolate Brownies *63*

Yellow Point Cranberry Cardamom Bars *65*

BY BREADS, I MEAN *DOUGHNUTS*! Well, not exclusively, but they are a quick bread and uber easy to make. All the recipes in this chapter are relatively uncomplicated and are guaranteed to please a crowd. Below are some guidelines to help you get the best results every time.

- Breads generally fall into one of two categories: yeasted and non-yeasted. Yeasted breads contain either baker's yeast or a natural, self-generated yeast such as sourdough. Non-yeasted breads contain other leaveners, such as baking powder, baking soda, or eggs, to give them body.
- If you're making a yeasted bread, be sure to note the rising time. You don't want to jump into a recipe expecting to serve it within the hour, only to discover the rising time is 2 hours or longer.
- Some of these recipes require deep-frying, so have a candy or frying thermometer on hand to monitor the temperature of the oil.
- Make sure your butter and eggs are at the temperature specified in the recipe, as their temperature can affect the rate at which breads rise and bars bake.
- When you're allowing bread to rise during the colder, winter months, you can turn your oven to 200°F (95°C) for 10 minutes, turn it off when it reaches temperature, wait 5 minutes without opening the oven door, and then let your dough rise in the oven in a mixing bowl with a tea towel over it.
- When you're making bars, you can use either butter or oil and flour or cocoa powder in your baking pan to ensure the bars come out cleanly, or place two strips of parchment at right angles (like a cross) across the bottom and up the sides of the pan.

Masala Chai Spiced Buttermilk Doughnuts

MAKES 24 DOUGHNUTS + 24 DOUGHNUT HOLES

Classic buttermilk doughnuts get a delicious kick of spice with the addition of some homemade masala chai. These doughnuts are so easy to make that you'll have them in constant rotation whenever you're looking for a decadent dessert. Be aware that these are yeasted doughnuts and require 45–60 minutes to rise.

2 tsp (10 mL) ground cinnamon
2 tsp (10 mL) ground ginger
1 tsp (5 mL) ground cardamom
½ tsp (2.5 mL) ground nutmeg
½ tsp (2.5 mL) ground cloves
½ tsp (2.5 mL) finely ground black pepper
1 Tbsp (15 mL) active dry yeast
½ cup (125 mL) warm water
2½–3 cups (625–750 mL) all-purpose flour
3 Tbsp (45 mL) granulated sugar
2 tsp (10 mL) baking powder
1 tsp (5 mL) fine sea salt
2 egg yolks, room temperature
½ cup (125 mL) buttermilk, room temperature
3 Tbsp (45 mL) unsalted butter, melted
Canola oil for frying
3 cups (750 mL) icing sugar
3–4 Tbsp (45–60 mL) strong-brewed chai

1. Line a baking sheet with parchment paper and sprinkle the parchment with a light dusting of flour.
2. In a small bowl, mix the cinnamon, ginger, cardamom, nutmeg, cloves, and black pepper together. Set this chai spice mix aside.
3. Using a stand mixer or a large mixing bowl, dissolve the yeast in the warm water and let stand for 5 minutes. Attach the bread hook to your mixer and add 2½ cups (625 mL) flour, sugar, baking powder, sea salt, 4 tsp (20 mL) of the chai spice mix, egg yolks, buttermilk, and melted butter. Turn the mixer to the lowest setting and knead until a soft dough forms, 1–2 minutes. Add more flour as needed, about ¼ cup (60 mL) at a time, so that the dough is nice and soft but not overly sticky.
4. On a lightly floured surface, roll the dough out to ½-inch (1.25 cm) thickness and cut the doughnut forms out with a doughnut cutter. If you don't have a doughnut cutter, use a floured glass with a 2½-inch (6.5 cm) diameter to cut out the basic shape and a large piping tip to cut out the centres for the doughnut holes. Place the doughnuts and doughnut holes on the prepared baking sheet and cover with a tea towel. Let rise until doubled in bulk, approximately 45 minutes.
5. Line a cooling rack with paper towel. Place parchment paper under another cooling rack.
6. Fit a large, deep-sided Dutch oven or stainless-steel pot with a thermometer and heat 3–4 inches (7.5–10 cm) of oil to 375°F (190°C). If you're using a deep fryer, set the machine to the same temperature. Fry 3 doughnuts and 3 holes at a time until golden, about 1 minute. Flip them over and continue to fry until they are evenly golden all over. Remove the doughnuts from the oil with a slotted spoon and set them on the paper towel-lined cooling rack to drain the excess oil.

7 In a shallow, wide-bottomed bowl or pan, combine the icing sugar, 3 Tbsp (45 mL) of chai, and the remaining chai spice, and whisk until smooth. The glaze should coat the back of a spoon but still be fluid enough to release excess. If it needs to be loosened a bit more, add the remaining 1 Tbsp (15 mL) of chai and whisk until smooth.

8 Dip each doughnut into the glaze while still warm, shake off the excess, and place on the second cooling rack to allow the glaze to dry.

9 Store in an airtight container at room temperature for up to 4 days.

Apple Rosemary Fritters

MAKES 6 LARGE OR 12 SMALL FRITTERS

Earthy-scented rosemary is the perfect companion to sweet, tart apples in these lighter-than-air fritters. They are best served warm and make the perfect morning coffee-time treat, as they whip up in a matter of minutes.

2 cups (500 mL) all-purpose flour
¼ cup (60 mL) granulated sugar
2 Tbsp (30 mL) finely chopped fresh rosemary
½ tsp (2.5 mL) baking powder
½ tsp (2.5 mL) fine sea salt
½ cup (125 mL) whole milk, cold
½ cup (125 mL) homemade or store-bought applesauce
2 eggs, whisked
1 tsp (5 mL) vanilla extract
2 large tart apples, peeled, cored, and diced
Canola oil for frying
2 cups (500 mL) icing sugar
¼ cup (60 mL) lemon juice

1. Line a cooling rack with paper towel. Place parchment paper under another cooling rack.
2. In a large mixing bowl, whisk together the flour, sugar, rosemary, baking powder, and salt. Add the milk, applesauce, eggs, and vanilla. Stir with a wooden spoon until the batter just comes together. Lightly fold in the apples, being sure not to over-mix.
3. In a high-sided Dutch oven, heavy pot, or deep fryer, heat 4 inches (10 cm) of oil to 350°F (175°C). Using a ¼-cup (60 mL) scoop and a kitchen spoon, carefully add the fritter batter to the hot oil. Fry 2 or 3 fritters at a time until they turn deeply golden brown, then flip to cook the other side, about 6–8 minutes per side. Use a slotted spoon to remove the fritters from the oil and place them on the paper towel-lined cooling rack to drain.
4. In a medium bowl, whisk together the icing sugar and lemon juice. Place some parchment or paper towel underneath a cooling rack and then, while the fritters are still warm, dip them into the glaze, turning to coat well. Shake off the excess and place them on the second cooling rack to dry fully.
5. Store the fritters in an airtight container at room temperature for up to 4 days.

Apple & Aged-Cheddar Scones

MAKES 8 SCONES

Fluffy, savoury, and a little bit sweet, these scones make use of the incredible apple harvest we get every year here on the farm and are the perfect finale to any meal. Serve them alongside a fruit platter with a salty blue cheese, pear or apple butter (page 162), or fig and apple compote (page 145).

- 2½ cups (625 mL) all-purpose flour
- 1 Tbsp (15 mL) baking powder
- ½ tsp (2.5 mL) fine sea salt
- ⅓ cup (80 mL) unsalted butter, cold, cut into 1-inch (2.5 cm) cubes
- 2 eggs, beaten
- ¾ cup (180 mL) whipping cream plus 2 Tbsp (30 mL) for brushing
- 1 cup (250 mL) shredded aged sharp cheddar
- 2 medium apples, skin on, cored, chopped into ½-inch (1.25 cm) cubes

1. Preheat the oven to 400°F (200°C). Line a baking sheet with parchment paper.
2. In a large mixing bowl, mix together the flour, baking powder, and salt. Add the butter and use a pastry cutter to cut it in until the mixture has the texture of coarse crumbs and small pieces of butter are just visible.
3. In a small bowl, whisk the eggs with the ¾ cup (180 mL) of cream to combine. Add this mixture to the dry ingredients and stir lightly with a wooden spoon or your hands until a loose dough forms. Turn the mixture out onto a lightly floured surface and knead the dough with your hands until it comes together. Press the mixture out into a flat 4- × 12-inch (10 × 30 cm) rectangle and scatter the cheese and apples across half of the dough. Fold the dough over itself to encase the cheese and apples and then continue to knead for another 10–12 strokes, or until the mixture is smooth.
4. Press or roll the dough into an 8-inch (20 cm) circle and cut it into 8 equal-sized wedges. Place the wedges 1 inch (2.5 cm) apart on the prepared baking sheet and brush the tops with the remaining 2 Tbsp (30 mL) of cream. Bake until the scones are evenly golden, 20–25 minutes. Remove the tray from the oven and place the scones on a cooling rack for 5 minutes. They are delicious served warm with butter.
5. The scones can be stored in an airtight container for 2–3 days at room temperature or up to 1 week in the refrigerator. They also freeze well and can be reheated at 350°F (175°C) for 10 minutes once thawed.

Chocolate, Cherry & Lemon Thyme Bread Pudding with Red Wine Reduction

SERVES 6–8

Bread pudding was a staple in my household when I was growing up, and it is the perfect canvas for almost any combination of fresh or dried fruit and spices or herbs. In this recipe, dark chocolate, sweet ripe cherries, and savoury lemon thyme are mixed with creamy custard and topped with a tangy red wine reduction for a deeply decadent dessert.

2 cups (500 mL) good quality red wine
1 cup (250 mL) granulated sugar, divided
1 tsp (5 mL) ground cinnamon
2 Tbsp (30 mL) unsalted butter, room temperature, plus more for greasing the baking dish
2 cups (500 mL) whole milk, cold
6 eggs
2 tsp (10 mL) vanilla extract
½ tsp (2.5 mL) fine sea salt
1 loaf challah, cut into 2-inch (5 cm) cubes (about 7–8 cups/1.75–2 L)
4 cups (1 L) fresh or frozen pitted cherries
1½ cups (375 mL) roughly chopped bittersweet chocolate
3 Tbsp (45 mL) fresh lemon thyme leaves

1. In a small, non-reactive saucepan, place the red wine, ½ cup (125 mL) of the sugar, and the cinnamon. Give the ingredients a stir to distribute and dissolve the sugar. Place the pot on medium-high heat and bring to a boil without stirring. Turn down the heat to low and continue to cook until reduced by half, approximately 30 minutes. The syrup is done when it coats the back of a spoon. Remove from the heat and set aside to cool to room temperature until needed. This is your red wine reduction sauce. It will keep in an airtight container at room temperature for up to 2 days or up to 3 weeks in the refrigerator.
2. Preheat the oven to 350°F (175°C). Butter a 9- × 13-inch (23 × 33 cm) baking dish well.
3. Melt the butter in a small saucepan over low heat and set aside to cool slightly. Using a stand mixer fitted with the whisk attachment (or a large mixing bowl and a handheld electric mixer), whisk the milk, eggs, vanilla, salt, and remaining ½ cup (125 mL) of sugar on medium speed for 2 minutes. Add the melted butter and whisk on high speed for 1 minute more, just to combine.
4. Remove the bowl from the stand mixer and add the bread cubes to the egg mixture. Using your hands, toss well so the bread soaks up much of the milky mixture. Add the cherries, chocolate, and lemon thyme, and toss again to distribute evenly. Pour the mixture into the prepared baking dish and bake until the custard is set but still a bit wobbly and the edges of the bread have turned a golden brown, 35–45 minutes.
5. Serve the bread pudding with the red wine reduction sauce and a good quality ice cream. Leftovers can be covered with plastic or beeswax wrap in the baking dish and kept in the refrigerator for up to 3 days.

Chocolate Walnut Zucchini Bread

MAKES 1 (4- × 8-INCH/10 × 20 CM) LOAF

Who said vegetables couldn't be served for dessert? Zucchini and walnuts both grow in abundance on our farm, and they come to harvest at the same time. The zucchini in this loaf adds an incredibly rich moistness to the deep chocolatey decadence of the bread. This recipe calls for extra-dark Dutch or black cocoa powder, but if you can't find that, regular Dutch cocoa will do. You can omit the walnuts if you prefer, but they do add a wonderful crunchy bite. I like to make this in a loaf pan, but you can also use a 9-inch (23 cm) square cake pan—just reduce the total baking time to 25 minutes.

- ⅓ cup plus 2 Tbsp (110 mL) unsalted butter, melted, divided
- ½ cup (125 mL) extra-dark Dutch processed cocoa, divided
- 1¼ cups (310 mL) all-purpose flour
- 1 cup (250 mL) granulated sugar
- 1 Tbsp (15 mL) espresso powder (optional)
- 1 tsp (5 mL) fine sea salt
- ¾ tsp (3.75 mL) baking soda
- ¾ tsp (3.75 mL) baking powder
- 1 cup (250 mL) walnuts, roughly chopped
- 1 cup (250 mL) semisweet chocolate chips, divided
- 2 large eggs, room temperature
- ¼ cup (60 mL) Greek yoghurt
- 2 tsp (10 mL) vanilla extract
- 1½ cups (375 mL) grated zucchini

1. Preheat the oven to 350°F (175°C). Brush a 4- × 8-inch (10 × 20 cm) loaf pan with 2 Tbsp (30 mL) of the melted butter and dust with 2 Tbsp (30 mL) of the cocoa powder. Turn the pan upside down and tap to shake off the excess cocoa. Set aside.
2. In a large bowl, whisk together the remaining cocoa powder with the flour, sugar, espresso powder (if using), salt, baking soda, and baking powder until combined. Mix in the walnuts and ¾ cup (180 mL) of the chocolate chips. Set aside.
3. In a separate bowl, whisk the remaining ⅓ cup (80 mL) melted butter with the eggs, yoghurt, and vanilla until combined. Pour these wet ingredients into the dry ingredients and gently fold with a wooden spoon to combine. Fold in the zucchini, pour into the loaf pan, and top with the remaining ¼ cup (60 mL) of chocolate chips.
4. Bake for 25 minutes. Remove the pan from the oven and cover with foil. Return to the oven and bake until a toothpick inserted in the centre comes out clean, 20–30 minutes. Remove the pan from the oven and set on a cooling rack for at least 1 hour. Remove the bread from the pan and let it cool to room temperature on the cooling rack. It will still be warm when you remove it from the pan, and that's okay. If you remove it when it's still hot, though, it will break, so it's important to let it sit for at least 1 hour, as indicated.
5. The bread can be stored in an airtight container at room temperature for 4 days or in the refrigerator for up to 1 week.

Dried-Fruit Soda Bread Biscotti

MAKES APPROXIMATELY 24 BISCOTTI

Every summer when the fruit starts to ripen, I get out my dehydrator and try to preserve as many seasonal flavours as I can. These sweet and savoury biscotti crackers—topped with aged cheddar, a salty blue cheese, or a soft double cream cheese and a spoon of jam—are one of my favourite ways to use dried fruit, and they make a wonderful addition to any after-dinner cheese plate. They also make a great snack all on their own.

2½ cups (625 mL) red fife or other whole wheat flour
1¾ cups (430 mL) all-purpose flour, plus more for dusting
1½ tsp (7.5 mL) baking soda
1½ tsp (7.5 mL) fine sea salt
1½ cups (375 mL) roughly chopped mixed dried fruit (such as, apples, figs, apricots, cherries, grapes)
2 cups (500 mL) buttermilk, cold

1. Preheat the oven to 425°F (220°C). Line a baking sheet with parchment paper.
2. In a large bowl, whisk together the flours, baking soda, and salt. Add the dried fruit and toss to combine. Pour in the buttermilk and, using a wooden spoon, stir until a loose dough forms. Sprinkle a work surface with flour and turn the dough out onto it. Using your hands, gently knead the dough 10–12 times. The dough should start to come together but still be quite sticky. Place the dough on the prepared baking tray and form a loaf approximately 1½ × 10 inches (3.75 × 25 cm). Use a serrated knife to cut a ¼-inch-deep (0.5 cm) slit lengthwise down the loaf.
3. Bake the bread for 20 minutes and then turn the oven down to 400°F (200°C). Continue to bake until the base of the bread sounds hollow when tapped in the middle, approximately 20 minutes. Remove the baking sheet from the oven and set the bread on a cooling rack to cool completely, at least 2 hours.
4. Preheat the oven to 375°F (190°C). Line a baking sheet with fresh parchment paper.
5. Using a serrated knife, cut the bread into even ½–¾-inch (1.25–1.8 cm) slices. Lay the slices in a single layer and bake until they start to turn golden brown, 10–15 minutes. Flip the slices over and bake for another 10–15 minutes. Remove the tray from the oven and transfer the biscotti to a cooling rack to cool completely.
6. Once cool, the biscotti can be stored in an airtight container in the refrigerator for up to 1 week. If they become soft, they can be reheated/dried again in the oven at 375°F (190°C) for 5 minutes.

Toasted Hazelnut Chocolate Brownies

MAKES APPROXIMATELY 12–16 BROWNIES

Hazelnuts grow well across much of Vancouver Island's Cowichan Valley and beyond, and they are one of my favourite harvests of the year. When fresh, ripe hazelnuts are toasted, they have a delightful way of somehow making chocolate taste even more chocolatey—so if you're a lover of deep, dark chocolate, these brownies of Aurelia's are for you! You can, of course, make them without the nuts, or sub in almonds, pecans, or walnuts if desired.

½ cup (125 mL) hazelnuts
1¼ cups (310 mL) granulated sugar
½ cup (125 mL) icing sugar
¾ cup (180 mL) all-purpose flour
⅔ cup (160 mL) Dutch processed cocoa powder
1 tsp (5 mL) espresso powder
½ tsp (2.5 mL) fine sea salt
2 large eggs, room temperature
½ cup (125 mL) canola or avocado oil
2 Tbsp (30 mL) whole milk
2 tsp (10 mL) vanilla extract
½ cup (125 mL) finely chopped dark chocolate

FROSTING

¼ cup (60 mL) melted unsalted butter
⅓ cup (80 mL) Dutch processed cocoa
2 cups (500 mL) icing sugar
3 Tbsp (45 mL) whole milk

1. Preheat the oven to 350°F (175°C). Grease an 8- × 8-inch (20 × 20 cm) baking pan.
2. Spread the hazelnuts in a single layer on a baking sheet and bake until lightly browned and fragrant, about 10 minutes. Remove from the oven and turn down the heat to 325°F (165°C).
3. Place the hazelnuts on a large, clean tea towel and fold the towel over itself, gathering all the sides at the top. Roll the nuts around in the tea towel to remove the skins. Open the towel and pick out the hazelnuts, discarding the pieces of skin. Set the nuts aside.
4. In a large mixing bowl, whisk together both sugars, the flour, cocoa powder, espresso powder, and salt. In another mixing bowl, whisk together the eggs, oil, milk, and vanilla. Add the dry ingredients to the wet and mix well with a wooden spoon until just combined. Fold in the dark chocolate and toasted hazelnuts.
5. Pour the batter into the prepared pan and bake until the centre of the brownies is just barely set but still has a little movement to it, 40–45 minutes. Remove the pan from the oven and place on a cooling rack to let the brownies cool completely.
6. Place the frosting ingredients together in the bowl of a stand mixer fitted with a whisk attachment and beat until smooth. Frost the cooled brownies immediately—the frosting will set and become firm. Cut brownies into bars or squares as desired.
7. Store in an airtight container at room temperature for up to 3 days or in the freezer for up to 3 months.

Yellow Point Cranberry Cardamom Bars

MAKES 16 BARS

Grinding your own spice mix is super easy and delivers much more flavour than any store-bought variety ever could. It helps to have a dedicated coffee grinder that you use specifically for spice; you can clean it in between uses by grinding a tablespoon of white rice. (You can store the ground rice in an airtight jar and use it to thicken and flavour gravy and sauces as needed.) In these bars, the toasted fragrant cardamom highlights the sour floral flavour of the cranberries grown at Yellow Point on Vancouver Island. You can mix up the flavours by replacing the cardamom with 2 whole star anise or 1 tablespoon (15 mL) of either black pepper or cloves, depending on your tastes.

3 whole cardamom pods
3 cups (750 mL) fresh or frozen Yellow Point or other cranberries
⅓ cup (80 mL) granulated sugar
⅓ cup (80 mL) freshly squeezed orange juice (1–2 oranges)
2 tsp (10 mL) cornstarch
2 cups (500 mL) rolled oats
1 cup (250 mL) all-purpose flour
½ cup (125 mL) packed light brown sugar
1 tsp (5 mL) ground cardamom (or 3 whole cardamom pods, toasted and ground)
¼ tsp (1.25 mL) baking powder
¼ tsp (1.25 mL) fine sea salt
¾ cup (180 mL) unsalted butter, softened, cubed
2 Tbsp (60 mL) whole milk
2 tsp (10 mL) vanilla extract

1 Preheat the oven to 350°F (175°C). Line an 8- × 8-inch (20 × 20 cm) baking dish with parchment paper.
2 Using the back of a knife, crack the whole cardamom pods slightly. Then, in a medium saucepan set over medium heat, mix together the pods, cranberries, sugar, orange juice, and cornstarch. Stirring often, cook until the mixture is thick and bubbly and the cranberries are completely broken down, about 10 minutes. Remove the mixture from the heat and remove the whole cardamom pods.
3 In a medium mixing bowl, whisk the oats, flour, sugar, ground cardamom, baking powder, and salt until well combined. Using your fingers, rub the butter into the mixture until it has the consistency of very coarse sand, then stir in the milk and vanilla.
4 Pour half of the oat mixture into the prepared dish and press down firmly with the back of a spoon to form a solid base. Pour the cranberry mixture over top and spread it evenly. Place the remaining oat mixture on top and press it down gently and evenly with the back of a spoon.
5 Bake until the top turns golden brown, 25–30 minutes. Remove the pan from the oven and let it cool on a wire cooling rack for at least 1 hour. Once cool, cut into 16 squares.
6 Store the bars in an airtight container in the refrigerator for up to 1 week.

Cakes, Cobblers & Crumbles

Blackberry Sponge Cake *73*

Ginger, Pear & Parsnip Cake *77*

Carrot Celebration Cake *81*

Summer Berry Sheet Cake *86*

Italian Plum & Thyme Crumble *89*

Brown Butter, Apple & Rosemary Cobbler *91*

Pumpkin-Spiced Tea Cake *93*

Buffalo Milk Cheesecake with Cranberry Compote *95*

WHENEVER WE CELEBRATE the *big* things in life, there is inevitably cake! Birthdays, weddings, and anniversaries of all sorts, all seem incomplete without this "king of desserts," and with Aurelia Louvet—cake creator extraordinaire—as my business partner, I firmly believe that delicious cakes should be eaten every day! Cobblers use a similar batter to cake and are a wonderful way to use up the abundance of fruit at harvest time, while crumbles offer a similar but gluten-free option with oats and sugar as their topping. Whatever your preference, the recipes included in this chapter are so quick and easy to put together that I'm sure they'll find their way into your dessert repertoire in no time. Here are some tips to help you get the most out of the recipes.

- Be sure that eggs and butter are at room temperature before you start.
- Be sure to evenly grease and flour cake pans to ensure cakes come out cleanly.
- Preheat the oven so it's at the correct temperature before the cake, cobbler, or crumble goes in. For cakes, it's important to get the correct hit of initial heat to begin the rising process. A cold oven can lead to flat results. Likewise, cobblers and crumbles need a properly preheated oven to set their toppings; otherwise the batter and butter will simply drain into the fruit.
- Once the batter is ready, pour it into the pan and bake right away to avoid separation of the ingredients.
- Do not open the oven until the first testing time given in the recipe. If you do, you risk lowering the oven temperature before the cake rises. The result will be a dense, flat cake instead of a light and fluffy one.
- Let cakes cool so that the pan is comfortable to touch before turning them out. As the cake cools, it will pull away from the pan, making for a cleaner and easier release.
- Once the cakes are out of the pan, let them come to room temperature and then, if you have the time, place them in the refrigerator for 1 hour before frosting to ensure the icing sticks well to the cake's surface.
- Cakes taste better at room temperature. Keep them under a cake lid so they don't dry out and will still taste delicious the day after you bake them.
- For cobblers and crumbles, chop the fruit into evenly sized pieces to ensure even cooking throughout.
- Let cobblers and crumbles rest for at least 20 minutes before serving! Fruit contains a lot of sugar and is molten hot when it comes out of the oven. If you let the crumble rest, you give the filling time to come together—and the crumble will be safe to serve.

Blackberry Sponge Cake

MAKES 1 (TWO-LAYER 8-INCH/20 CM) CAKE

This traditional Victoria sponge recipe has been passed down to me through my British family and is a much-loved summer classic in our house. Here it gets a West Coast makeover with the juiciest of late-summer fruits, the delicious blackberry! While some consider the bramble to be the "king" of all berries, blueberries, raspberries, tayberries, and classic strawberries all work equally well.

JAM

4 cups (1 L) fresh or frozen blackberries
1 cup (250 mL) granulated sugar
2 tsp (10 mL) grated lemon zest

CREAM

2 cups (500 mL) whipping cream
2 Tbsp (30 mL) icing sugar
1 tsp (5 mL) vanilla extract

CAKE

1 cup (250 mL) unsalted butter, room temperature
1 cup (250 mL) granulated sugar
4 large eggs, room temperature
2 Tbsp (30 mL) whole milk
1½ Tbsp (22.5 mL) vanilla extract
1¾ cups (430 mL) self-rising flour
2 dozen blackberries
Icing sugar for dusting

JAM

1 Place all the ingredients in a small, non-reactive pot over medium heat. Cook for 5 minutes, stirring frequently, to mix in the sugar and break down the blackberries. Once all the sugar is dissolved, turn down the heat to medium-low and cook for 10 minutes, stirring occasionally to break up the fruit. Remove the pot from the heat and set aside to cool.
2 Once the jam has cooled for 15 minutes, transfer it to a 2-cup (500 mL) wide-mouth mason jar or ceramic bowl and let it sit to cool completely. Cover and refrigerate until needed.

CREAM

1 Using a stand mixer fitted with a paddle attachment (or a large mixing bowl and a handheld electric mixer), beat the cream, icing sugar, and vanilla extract on low speed until the ingredients are incorporated, about 1 minute. Turn the speed up to high and whip until the cream becomes quite stiff, 3–5 minutes. You'll know it's ready when stiff peaks appear when you remove the beaters from the bowl. Stop there, or you risk splitting the cream and having butter instead of whipped cream.
2 Transfer to an airtight container and store in the refrigerator until needed. >

CAKE

1. Preheat the oven to 350°F (175°C). Generously grease and flour two 8-inch (20 cm) round cake pans and line the bottoms with parchment paper.
2. Using a stand mixer fitted with a paddle attachment (or a mixing bowl and a handheld electric mixer), beat the butter and sugar on medium-low speed until the mixture is light and very fluffy, 4–5 minutes. Add the eggs one at a time, mixing well between additions, and beat until just combined. Mix in the milk and vanilla. Add the flour in two additions and mix on low speed until just combined.
3. Divide the batter between the prepared cake pans and smooth the tops. Gently tap the pans on the counter several times to release excess air bubbles. Bake the cakes until they are golden and a toothpick inserted into the middle comes out clean, 20–25 minutes. Place the pans on cooling racks and let the cakes cool completely.

ASSEMBLY

1. Remove one cake from the pan and place it on a serving platter. Remove the blackberry jam and whipped cream from the refrigerator and loosely fold them together. You don't want to mix them completely; you just want to create a swirly mass of jammy cream. Place a couple of large scoops of the jammy cream on the cake base. It should be about 1½ inches (3.75 cm) thick. Dot the cream with half of the fresh blackberries. This will help hold the upper layer in place. Place the other cake on top. Use a bench scraper to smooth the cream around the outside edges of the cake. Dust the top of the cake with icing sugar and garnish with the remaining cream and blackberries.
2. The cake and cream can be stored, covered, for 3–4 days in the refrigerator.

Ginger, Pear & Parsnip Cake

MAKES 1 (9- × 9-INCH/23 × 23 CM) CAKE + 2 CUPS (500 ML) CARAMEL

While the ingredient list may look long and daunting, do not be afraid! This is one of the easiest cakes in this book to make, and it's absolutely worth the effort. And if parsnips in a cake seems odd to you, have faith—much like carrots, they lend the perfect amount of moist earthiness to complement the sweet spice of the ginger and pears.

CAKE

½ cup (125 mL) unsalted butter, room temperature, cubed
¾ cup (180 mL) packed dark brown sugar, divided
2 Tbsp (30 mL) finely chopped candied ginger in syrup
4 medium pears
2 eggs, room temperature, whisked
1 cup (250 mL) unsalted butter, melted and cooled slightly
½ cup (125 mL) buttermilk, cold
½ cup (125 mL) unsulphured fancy grade molasses
1 tsp (5 mL) vanilla extract
2¼ cups (560 mL) red fife flour
½ tsp (2.5 mL) baking soda
½ tsp (2.5 mL) baking powder
½ tsp (2.5 mL) fine sea salt
1½ tsp (7.5 mL) ground ginger
1 tsp (5 mL) ground cinnamon
½ tsp (2.5 mL) ground cloves
¼ tsp (1.25 mL) ground nutmeg
1 cup (250 mL) peeled and finely grated parsnip

CARAMEL

1 cup (250 mL) granulated sugar
1 cup (250 mL) whipping cream
2 Tbsp (30 mL) unsalted butter
2 Tbsp (30 mL) good quality rum or brandy, optional
½ tsp (2.5 mL) flaky sea salt

CAKE

1 Preheat the oven to 350°F (175°C). Lightly grease a 9- × 9-inch (23 × 23 cm) baking pan.
2 Melt the ½ cup (125 mL) of butter in a small saucepan over low heat. Remove from the heat and stir in ¼ cup (60 mL) of the brown sugar and the chopped candied ginger. Set aside.
3 Peel, core, and slice the pears lengthwise into ½-inch-thick (1.25 cm) slices and arrange as desired in the bottom of the cake pan. We like to overlap them in a pretty pattern. Pour the butter and ginger mixture over the pears and set aside.
4 Using a stand mixer fitted with a paddle attachment (or a large bowl and a handheld electric mixer), mix the eggs, melted butter, buttermilk, molasses, and vanilla together on low speed until combined, about 1 minute. Turn the speed to medium-high and whisk until well combined and slightly lighter in colour, about 3 minutes.

>

5. In a separate bowl, whisk together the flour, baking soda, baking powder, salt, ground ginger, cinnamon, cloves, and nutmeg. Add the dry ingredients to the wet ingredients and mix on low speed until just combined, 1–2 minutes. Fold in the grated parsnips until fully mixed in and then pour the batter over the pears. Bake until a toothpick inserted into the centre of the cake comes out clean, 35–40 minutes. Remove the cake from the oven and let it stand in the pan on a cooling rack for 10–15 minutes before inverting onto a serving platter.

CARAMEL

1. Place the granulated sugar in a non-reactive, heavy-bottomed, high-sided saucepan over medium heat. As the sugar starts to melt and caramelize, pick the pot up off the heat and swirl to mix. Do not stir. Return to the heat and continue to melt the sugar, swirling every few seconds, until it is all melted and has turned a deep golden colour.
2. Remove the pot from the heat and carefully add the whipping cream to the sugar. It will bubble up rapidly, so be very careful as you do this. Once all the cream has been added, stir quickly with a wooden spoon until the bubbling has subsided. Don't worry if it seems like you have a solid mass of sugar in a pool of cream. Add the butter, rum or brandy (if using), and salt and place the pot over medium heat again. Continue to cook while stirring with a wooden spoon until all the ingredients have melted and combined to form a smooth liquid caramel. Cook for another 3–5 minutes to reduce and thicken and then remove the pot from the heat. Let it cool slightly before serving.
3. To serve, drizzle a spoonful of caramel onto a serving plate and top with a slice of cake.
4. The cake can be stored covered for 3–4 days at room temperature. The caramel will last for up to 2 weeks in a glass jar in the refrigerator. To serve, bring it to room temperature on the counter or reheat slightly in the microwave.

Carrot Celebration Cake

MAKES 1 (FOUR-LAYER, 8-INCH/20 CM) CAKE

Whenever people ask me whether I prefer chocolate or vanilla cake, I always reply, *Carrot!* Made with sweet, late-summer garden carrots, this is my go-to for every important celebration. If you're not a fan of coconut, it's okay to leave it out, but be sure to include the pineapple, as it makes the cake extra moist and delicious.

CAKE

3 large eggs, room temperature
1 cup (250 mL) granulated sugar
½ cup (125 mL) extra virgin olive oil
½ cup (125 mL) buttermilk, room temperature
2 tsp (10 mL) vanilla extract
2 cups (500 mL) self-rising flour
2 tsp (10 mL) ground cinnamon
1 tsp (5 mL) ground ginger
½ tsp (2.5 mL) ground cloves
½ tsp (2.5 mL) ground nutmeg
2 cups (500 mL) grated carrots
1 cup (250 mL) shredded unsweetened coconut, lightly toasted
1 (8 oz/225 g) can crushed pineapple with juice

CREAM CHEESE FROSTING

16 oz (450 g) block-style cream cheese, softened, cubed
1 cup (250 mL) unsalted butter, softened, cubed
1 Tbsp (15 mL) whipping cream
2 tsp (10 mL) vanilla extract
½ tsp (2.5 mL) fine sea salt
8 cups (2 L) icing sugar

CAKE

1 Preheat the oven to 350°F (175°C). Butter and flour the sides of two 8-inch (20 cm) round cake pans and line the bottoms with parchment paper.

2 Using a stand mixer fitted with a paddle attachment (or a large mixing bowl and a handheld electric mixer), mix the eggs, sugar, oil, buttermilk, and vanilla on medium-high speed until well combined. Add the flour and spices and beat on low speed until just combined. Be careful not to over-mix. Add the grated carrots, coconut, and crushed pineapple with juice and mix together by hand until well combined.

3 Pour the batter evenly into the prepared cake pans and bake until a toothpick inserted in the centre of each cake comes out clean, 35–40 minutes. Allow the cakes to cool in the pan for about 10 minutes and then run a knife carefully around the edges. Invert each cake onto a cooling rack and allow to cool completely in the refrigerator before frosting. >

CREAM CHEESE FROSTING

1 Using a stand mixer fitted with a paddle attachment (or a large mixing bowl and a handheld electric mixer), beat the cream cheese, butter, cream, vanilla, and salt on medium-high speed until the mixture is well combined and lump-free. Turn the mixer to low and add the icing sugar 1 cup (250 mL) at a time until it's all incorporated. Turn the mixer to high and continue to beat until the mixture is light and fluffy, about 1 minute.

2 Place the frosting in an airtight container in the refrigerator for 15–30 minutes to firm up before decorating the cake.

ASSEMBLY

1 Once the cakes are completely cooled, slice each one in half horizontally to create four layers. Place the first layer on a platter and, using an offset spatula, spread ½ cup (125 mL) of the frosting all the way to the edges of the cake. Repeat with the remaining three cake layers. Cover the top layer with frosting and spread it down the sides of the cake.

2 The cake can be stored under a cake lid for up to 3 days at room temperature or wrapped and refrigerated for up to 1 week.

Summer Berry Sheet Cake

MAKES 1 (9- × 13-INCH/23 × 33 CM) CAKE

After a long, dark West Coast winter of desserts made with dried, preserved, and frozen fruits, berry season hits the palate with an explosion of freshness. Whether you serve this cake frosted or with the icing on the side, the summer berries shine through, making it a great addition to any celebration. If you are making this out of season and need to use frozen berries, thaw and drain them in a sieve before using. Keep the juice to stain the icing if desired.

CAKE

2 cups (500 mL) all-purpose flour
1 tsp (5 mL) baking powder
1 tsp (5 mL) baking soda
½ tsp (2.5 mL) fine sea salt
½ cup (125 mL) almond flour
1 cup (250 mL) granulated sugar
½ cup (125 mL) extra virgin olive oil
3 eggs, room temperature
½ cup (125 mL) whole milk
¼ cup (60 mL) Greek yoghurt
1 Tbsp (15 mL) vanilla extract
1 tsp (5 mL) apple cider vinegar
1¼ cups (310 mL) strawberries, washed, dried, and quartered
1 cup (250 mL) raspberries, washed and dried
¾ cup (180 mL) blueberries, washed and dried

ICING

1 cup (250 mL) unsalted butter, room temperature
¼ cup (60 mL) freeze-dried berry powder (page 163)
½ tsp (2.5 mL) fine sea salt
4 cups (1 L) icing sugar
3 Tbsp (45 mL) whipping cream
1 Tbsp (15 mL) vanilla extract

CAKE

1 Preheat the oven to 350°F (175°C). Butter and flour a 9- × 13-inch (23 × 33 cm) baking pan. Set aside.
2 In a medium mixing bowl, sieve the all-purpose flour, baking powder, baking soda, and salt. Add the almond flour and stir to combine. Set aside.
3 Using a stand mixer fitted with a paddle attachment (or a large mixing bowl and a handheld electric mixer), mix the sugar and olive oil on medium speed until the sugar is completely dissolved, 3–5 minutes. Add the 3 eggs and beat on high speed until the mixture has slightly lightened in colour, about 3 minutes. Add the milk, yoghurt, vanilla, and vinegar, and mix together for another minute on medium speed to combine. Add half of the dry ingredients to the mixing bowl and mix on low until just combined. Add the remaining dry ingredients and mix again until the batter is just combined. Do not over-mix.
4 Pour the batter into the prepared cake pan and then scatter the berries across the top of the cake. Do not mix them in. Bake until a toothpick inserted into the middle of the cake comes out clean, 30–35 minutes. Remove the pan from the oven and place on a cooling rack to cool to room temperature.
5 Place in the refrigerator for an additional 30 minutes before frosting.

ICING

1. Using a stand mixer fitted with a paddle attachment (or a large mixing bowl and a handheld electric mixer), mix the butter, berry powder, and salt on high speed for about 2 minutes, just to combine. Sift in the icing sugar 1 cup (250 mL) at a time, beating on low speed for 1 minute after each addition. Scrape down the sides of the bowl and beat for another minute. Add 1 Tbsp (15 mL) of the cream and then add the vanilla. Beat until you have an even, fluffy consistency, 2–3 minutes. If the frosting is slightly too stiff to spread easily, add the remaining cream, 1 Tbsp (15 mL) at a time, until the frosting has a thick but spreadable consistency.
2. Ice the cake while it's still in the pan and then slice and serve.
3. The cake will keep, covered, in the pan for up to 3 days in the refrigerator.

Italian Plum & Thyme Crumble

SERVES 4–6

Sweet, tart Italian plums marry perfectly with the savoury scent of freshly picked thyme in this crumble, one of my favourite summer desserts. This dish comes together in about 20 minutes and can be popped in the oven while you're eating dinner so that it's ready when you are. You can wrap any leftover or even pre-made crumble tightly in plastic or in an airtight container and keep it in the freezer for up to 3 months. Thaw fully before baking as described below.

FILLING

3½ lb (1.6 kg) Italian plums, quartered and stones discarded
¼ cup (60 mL) packed light brown sugar
2 Tbsp (30 mL) fresh thyme leaves
1 Tbsp (15 mL) cornstarch
Grated zest of 1 lemon
2 tsp (10 mL) vanilla extract
Pinch of fine sea salt

CRUMBLE TOPPING

½ cup (125 mL) almond flour
½ cup (125 mL) whole oats
¼ cup (60 mL) granulated sugar
¼ cup (60 mL) packed light brown sugar
2 Tbsp (30 mL) fresh thyme leaves
1 tsp (5 mL) freshly ground black pepper
6 Tbsp (90 mL) unsalted butter, melted

1 Preheat the oven to 375°F (190°C).

FILLING

1 Place the plums, sugar, thyme, cornstarch, lemon zest, vanilla, and salt in a bowl and toss together until well combined.
2 Tip the mixture into a 6- × 9- × 3-inch (15 × 23 × 7.5 cm) glass or ceramic baking dish and set aside.

CRUMBLE TOPPING

1 In a separate bowl, place the flour, oats, both sugars, thyme, and pepper. Toss to combine. Pour in the melted butter and mix well until the mixture is uniform and there are no dry patches of flour.
2 Place the crumble mixture evenly on top of the plums and bake until the fruit is bubbly and the topping is golden brown, 25–30 minutes. Let sit for at least 15–30 minutes before serving, as the fruit will be scalding hot.
3 Leftovers can be stored in an airtight container in the refrigerator for up to 5 days.

Brown Butter, Apple & Rosemary Cobbler

SERVES 9–12

The tastes of apple and rosemary embody autumn on the West Coast islands, and this cobbler brings them together with the rich, toasted notes of browned butter. This cobbler pairs beautifully with Roasted Chestnut Ice Cream (page 147) or Fig & Apple Ice Cream (page 145).

1 cup (250 mL) apple cider
2 Tbsp (30 mL) lemon juice
1 tsp (5 mL) vanilla extract
½ cup (125 mL) packed dark brown sugar
1 Tbsp (15 mL) cornstarch
3 Tbsp (45 mL) finely chopped fresh rosemary
1 tsp (5 mL) ground cinnamon
¼ tsp (1.25 mL) fine sea salt
6 medium, tart baking apples, peeled and cut into ½-inch (1.25 cm) chunks
5 Tbsp (75 mL) unsalted butter
1 cup (250 mL) all-purpose flour
¾ cup (180 mL) granulated sugar
2 tsp (10 mL) baking powder
¼ tsp (1.25 mL) fine sea salt
¾ cup (180 mL) buttermilk, cold

1. Preheat the oven to 375°F (190°C).
2. In a 9-inch (23 cm) cast iron pan, mix together the apple cider, lemon juice, vanilla, brown sugar, cornstarch, rosemary, cinnamon, and salt. Stir in the apples and cook over medium heat for 3–5 minutes, stirring regularly. Once the liquid begins to form simmering bubbles constantly, remove the pan from the heat and set aside.
3. Place the butter in a large skillet over medium heat. Once it has melted, continue to cook, stirring constantly, until the butter turns a deep golden brown and has a nutty scent, 5–8 minutes. Remove from the heat immediately. Browned butter can burn quickly, so be sure to pay attention. Set aside to cool slightly.
4. In a large mixing bowl, mix together the flour, granulated sugar, baking powder, and salt. Using a wooden spoon, stir in the buttermilk and the cooled browned butter. Mix everything until just combined. Place the cobbler batter over the apples in large dollops and then bake until a toothpick inserted into the topping comes out clean, 18–25 minutes.
5. Remove from the oven and allow to cool for at least 10 minutes before serving.

Pumpkin-Spiced Tea Cake

MAKES 1 BUNDT CAKE

Does anything announce the arrival of autumn more than the appearance of all things pumpkin spice? This cake is no exception, transforming the flavour of my favourite coffee drink into a delicious Bundt cake, perfectly topped with spicy, creamy cinnamon glaze.

CAKE

2¼ cups (560 mL) self-rising flour

2 medium eggs

1 cup (250 mL) granulated sugar

1 cup (250 mL) buttermilk

¾ cup (180 mL) pumpkin purée (not pumpkin pie filling)

1 tsp (5 mL) vanilla extract

2 tsp (10 mL) pumpkin spice mix

1 tsp (5 mL) freshly ground black pepper

½ tsp (2.5 mL) fine sea salt

CINNAMON GLAZE

4 cups (1 L) icing sugar

½ cup (125 mL) Greek yoghurt

½ cup (125 mL) cream cheese, softened, cubed

1 tsp (5 mL) lemon juice

1 tsp (5 mL) ground cinnamon

CAKE

1. Preheat the oven to 350°F (175°C).
2. Using a fine mesh sieve, sift the flour into a large mixing bowl.
3. Using a stand mixer fitted with a paddle attachment (or a large, high-sided mixing bowl and a handheld electric mixer), beat the eggs and sugar on high speed until the mixture turns light yellow and starts to thicken, about 5 minutes.
4. Add the buttermilk, pumpkin purée, vanilla, pumpkin spice, pepper, and salt, and mix on medium speed until the ingredients all come together, about 30 seconds. Add the sifted flour to the pumpkin mixture and carefully mix together with a wooden spoon until the flour is just incorporated. Do not over-mix.
5. Pour the batter into a non-stick Bundt pan and bake until a skewer inserted into the centre comes out clean and the cake bounces back if you apply light pressure to the surface, 45–60 minutes. Place the pan on a cooling rack and let the cake cool completely.

CINNAMON GLAZE

1. Add all the glaze ingredients to the bowl of a stand mixer fitted with a paddle attachment. Beat on low speed until all the icing sugar is dissolved. Turn the speed to medium-high and beat until the glaze is smooth. Pour over the cooled cake.
2. The cake will keep covered at room temperature for 3–4 days and up to 1 week in the refrigerator.

Buffalo Milk Cheesecake with Cranberry Compote

MAKES 1 (9-INCH/23 CM) CHEESECAKE

If you haven't tried the water buffalo yoghurt from McClintock's Farm, you're missing out! Tart and unbelievably creamy, it gives this cheesecake a huge punch of flavour alongside the tangy, citrusy cranberry compote. For a summer twist, use the strawberry compote from the Strawberry Greens Panna Cotta recipe (page 157).

CHEESECAKE

2 cups (500 mL) gingersnap cookie crumbs (about 30 gingersnap cookies)
⅓ cup (80 mL) granulated sugar
½ tsp (2.5 mL) ground ginger
½ tsp (2.5 mL) freshly ground pepper
⅛ tsp (0.8 mL) fine sea salt
½ cup (125 mL) melted unsalted butter
4 large eggs, room temperature
1 Tbsp (15 mL) lemon juice
1 tsp (5 mL) pure vanilla extract
32 oz (907 g) full-fat, block-style cream cheese, room temperature, cubed
1½ cups (375 mL) granulated sugar
2 Tbsp (30 mL) cornstarch
1 cup (250 mL) plain buffalo milk yoghurt, room temperature

COMPOTE

2 cups (500 mL) fresh or frozen cranberries
1 cup (250 mL) freshly squeezed orange juice (about 4 oranges)
3 Tbsp (45 mL) grated orange zest
3 Tbsp (45 mL) packed dark brown sugar
½ tsp (2.5 mL) ground cinnamon
½ tsp (2.5 mL) ground cloves
¼ tsp (1.25 mL) ground nutmeg
¼ tsp (1.25 mL) fine sea salt

CHEESECAKE

1 Preheat the oven to 350°F (175°C). Lightly coat the inside of a 9-inch (23 cm) springform cake pan with butter.
2 In a small bowl, use your hands to mix together the cookie crumbs, sugar, ginger, pepper, salt, and melted butter. Combine until you have the texture of wet sand, then pour the mixture into the cake pan. Using your hands and/or a small measuring cup, firmly press the crust mixture down into the bottom and up the sides of the pan until it is evenly distributed and reaches almost to the top of the pan. Bake for 10 minutes to set the crust and then set aside on a cooling rack to cool while you prepare the filling.
3 In a small bowl, use a fork to mix together the eggs, lemon juice, and vanilla. Set aside.
4 Using a stand mixer fitted with a paddle attachment (or a bowl and an electric handheld mixer), beat the cream cheese on medium-low speed until smooth, about 1 minute. Add the sugar and cornstarch and mix on low to combine, about 30 seconds. Scrape the sides and bottom of the bowl with a rubber spatula and then mix again until well combined, approximately 30 seconds. With the mixer running on the lowest setting, add the egg mixture and the yoghurt. Mix on low for 1 minute to combine.

>

5 Preheat the oven to 300°F (150°C).
6 Pour the filling into the cooled crumb base and tap the pan on the counter a couple of times to remove any air bubbles. Place the cheesecake on the centre rack of the oven and place a casserole dish filled two-thirds of the way up with water on the bottom rack.
7 Bake for 1 hour, 40 minutes. Top up the water in the casserole dish after 1 hour if necessary. Turn off the oven, crack the door open an inch or two (2.5–5 cm), and let the cheesecake sit for another hour. Place the cooled cheesecake in the refrigerator, uncovered, and let it chill for at least 4 hours before serving.

COMPOTE

1 Mix together all the compote ingredients in a medium, non-reactive pot and place over medium heat. Stir occasionally with a wooden spoon until the mixture begins to bubble.
2 Turn the heat to medium-low and continue to stir occasionally, pressing down on the cranberries to crush them. Once all the berries have broken down, remove the pot from the heat and let it sit for 20 minutes. Pour the cooled compote into a jar fitted with a lid and store in the refrigerator for at least an hour.

ASSEMBLY

1 When you're ready to serve, crack open the springform pan and run a knife carefully around the edge of the crust before releasing fully. Serve with cranberry compote on the side.
2 The cheesecake, wrapped lightly in plastic or beeswax wrap, and the jarred compote will each keep separately in the refrigerator for up to 1 week.

Pies & Pastries

Flaky Pie Crust *104*

Peach & Basil Pie *107*

Stargazer Pie *109*

Apple Cheddar Rosemary Pie *113*

Spiced Plum Tarte Tatin *115*

Raspberry Meringue Pie *119*

Spiced Chai Napoleons *121*

Five-Spice Cherry Hand Pies *126*

Caramelized Peach & Herbed Ricotta Crêpes *129*

THE KEY TO A SUCCESSFUL PIE is a light, flaky, yet crispy pastry to hold whatever delicious filling you choose. Practice makes perfect here, and I have a few key tips that can help you be successful straight out of the gate. While making your own Flaky Pie Crust (page 104) is simple, store-bought varieties for both pie crusts and puff pastry can expedite and simplify the process.

- Unlike cakes and cookies, pastry needs all the ingredients to be as cold as possible. Butter, water, and even the flour can be kept in the refrigerator to ensure they stay chilled until you need them.
- If you don't have a food processor, grate frozen butter into the dry ingredients to distribute the fat more precisely.
- Don't skip the resting phase. Pastry needs time to rest and come together in the refrigerator after it's been formed. Wrap the dough tightly in plastic wrap and let it sit in the refrigerator for at least 1 hour, or up to overnight. The flour will continue to absorb the moisture while it rests, making your pastry easier to roll out.
- Pie plates do not need greasing. The butter in the pastry will allow your slices to come out cleanly.
- Place fruit pies on baking sheets before placing them in the oven. Any juice drippings will fall onto the baking tray and save you from cleaning burnt sugar out of your oven.
- Pies have an initial higher bake temperature than most desserts. This allows the crust to set and become crispy, even when using wet fillings. You can turn the temperature down halfway through the baking time or protect the crust from burning with a layer of aluminum foil if necessary.
- Wet the bottom edge of the pie pastry with a tiny bit of water before topping with the second layer. This will ensure a tight seal between the two when they are crimped together.
- Be sure to vent the top of double-crusted fruit pies. This will give the boiling fruit juices a convenient place to send their steam, so it won't pour out between the two pastry layers.
- Let fruit pies rest at least 25–30 minutes before serving. The fruit needs time to cool to a safe temperature and set into a sliceable structure.

Flaky Pie Crust

MAKES 1 (9-INCH/23 CM) DOUBLE PIE CRUST

Don't be daunted by the thought of making your own pie pastry. It's beyond easy with a food processor, as the machine does all the work for you. Be sure your butter is very cold and your water has ice in it, mix just until the pastry comes together, and let the pastry rest before rolling—that's it! Once you've mastered the basic recipe, try adding some of the flavour variations to take your pies to the next level.

BASIC CRUST

2¼ cups (560 mL) all-purpose flour
1 tsp (5 mL) fine sea salt
1 tsp (5 mL) baking powder
1 cup (250 mL) unsalted butter, frozen, grated with a large box grater, and then held in the freezer until needed
1 tsp (5 mL) white vinegar
8–10 Tbsp (120–150 mL) ice water

ADDITIONS FOR VARIATIONS

1 Tbsp (15 mL) dried or 2 Tbsp (30 mL) chopped fresh herbs, such as thyme, oregano, or rosemary, or a mix
2 tsp (10 mL) chai spice (see page 46)
2 tsp (10 mL) 5 spice (see page 126)
¼ cup (60 mL) grated aged cheddar
2 Tbsp (30 mL) Dutch processed cocoa

NOTE: Use only one set of variations per batch of pastry.

1 Place the flour, salt, baking powder, butter, and any additions in the bowl of a food processor fitted with a steel blade. Pulse until the mixture resembles coarse sand with some small, pea-sized lumps of butter, 15–20 seconds. If you don't have a food processor, grate frozen butter into the flour mixture to distribute the fat evenly.

2 Mix the vinegar and the ice water, then add to the food processor 1 Tbsp (15 mL) at a time, pulsing four or five times after each addition. The dough is done when it begins to form large clumps and pulls away from the sides of the food processor bowl.

3 Dump the mixture out onto a lightly floured work surface and, using your hands, push it together into a rough ball. Divide the dough in half and shape it into evenly sized discs. Wrap each disc tightly in plastic wrap and place in the refrigerator to rest and chill for at least 1 hour, or up to overnight.

4 When you're ready to make your pie crust, take the dough out of the refrigerator and let it rest for 5 minutes to begin to soften.

5 Lightly flour your work surface and a rolling pin, and roll out each disc, starting from the centre and pushing out toward the edge. Rotate the dough a quarter turn and repeat until your crust is approximately 12–13 inches (30–33 cm) in diameter. If the dough begins to stick, scatter a little bit of flour across the counter and the pastry disc. If the edges start to crack, pinch them together and roll over the seal with the rolling pin.

6 Once the crust is done, fold one piece in half, and then in half again so that it resembles a pie wedge. Place the point of the wedge in the centre of your pie plate and carefully unfold.
7 Add the second crust once the filling has been added. Flute (fold the edge under itself and, using your fingers, create an up and down pattern), trim and press with a fork, or apply as directed in your recipe.
8 Pies can be stored, covered, in the refrigerator for up to 5 days.

Peach & Basil Pie

MAKES 1 (9-INCH/23 CM) PIE

If ever a pie had the taste of summer baked into it, it must be this one! Juicy ripe peaches married with fragrant, floral basil is one of the most delicious flavour combinations around, and as both come into harvest simultaneously here on the islands, we get to enjoy this every time stone fruit season rolls around. Frozen peaches will work as well, so if you have an abundance of peaches in the summer, stash some away in the freezer for whenever the craving for this pie hits.

20 fresh basil leaves
8–9 fresh peaches, peeled and cut into 1-inch (2.5 cm) chunks
½ cup (125 mL) packed Demerara sugar
¼ cup (60 mL) granulated sugar
⅓ cup (80 mL) all-purpose flour
2 Tbsp (30 mL) cornstarch
½ tsp (2.5 mL) fine sea salt
3 Tbsp (45 mL) lemon juice
1 tsp (5 mL) vanilla extract
2 Tbsp (30 mL) unsalted butter, melted and cooled slightly
1 recipe Flaky Pie Crust (page 104)
1 egg yolk
1 Tbsp (15 mL) water
1 Tbsp (15 mL) coarse cane sugar

1 Preheat the oven to 400°F (200°C).
2 Place the basil leaves one on top of the other to form a stack, and then roll them together to form a tube. Using a sharp paring knife, chiffonade the basil: slice it finely across the tube to create long, fine strips of basil. Set aside.
3 Place the peach chunks in a large mixing bowl. Add both sugars, the flour, the cornstarch, and the salt. Toss to combine. Add the lemon juice, vanilla extract, and melted butter and toss again. Add the basil and toss again so that all the ingredients are evenly combined.
4 Line a 9-inch (23 cm) pie dish with one half of the pastry. Pour the pie filling into the crust and then add the top layer of pastry. You can use either a full top with crimped edges and vents on top, or you can create a lattice top.
5 Whisk the egg yolk and the water together in a small bowl, brush it across the top of the pie, and then sprinkle with the cane sugar. Place the pie on a baking sheet and bake on the centre rack of the oven for 20 minutes. Turn down the heat to 350°F (175°C) and bake until the crust has turned golden and the juices begin to bubble up through the top crust, 35–40 minutes. Remove the pie from the oven and let it rest on a cooling rack for at least an hour before serving.
6 The pie will keep, covered, in the refrigerator for 7–10 days.

Stargazer Pie

MAKES 1 (9-INCH/23 CM) PIE

This pie gets its name from the inky dark colour of haskap berries mixed with blackberries and blueberries—like a starry, moonless night on the islands. Haskaps give the filling a distinctive flavour. They have a more savoury note than the other two berries, with hints of rosemary and thyme, even without adding the herbs. If you can't find haskaps, increase the volume of the blueberries and blackberries by 1 cup (250 mL) each.

½ cup (125 mL) granulated sugar
⅓ cup (80 mL) cornstarch
2 Tbsp (30 mL) flour
1 tsp (5 mL) ground cinnamon
½ tsp (2.5 mL) fine sea salt
1 Tbsp (15 mL) grated lemon zest
2 cups (500 mL) fresh or frozen blueberries
2 cups (500 mL) fresh or frozen blackberries
2 cups (500 mL) fresh or frozen haskap berries
2 Tbsp (30 mL) Merridale Blackberry Liqueur (optional)
2 Tbsp (30 mL) lemon juice
2 Tbsp (30 mL) unsalted butter, melted
1 recipe Flaky Pie Crust (page 104)
1 egg yolk
1 Tbsp (15 mL) water
1 Tbsp (15 mL) coarse cane sugar

1. Preheat the oven to 400°F (200°C).
2. In a large mixing bowl, whisk together the sugar, cornstarch, flour, cinnamon, and salt. Use your fingers to rub in the lemon zest, making sure you distribute it evenly. Add the berries and, if using, the blackberry liqueur. Toss gently to coat. Drizzle in the lemon juice and melted butter, and then toss once more to combine evenly.
3. Line a 9-inch (23 cm) pie dish with one half of the pastry. Pour the berry filling into the dish and set it aside. Roll out the top layer of pastry to form a 12-inch (30 cm) circle. Using a 1- to 2-inch (2.5–5 cm) star-shaped cookie cutter, cut out several stars from the pie pastry, cutting no closer than 2 inches (5 cm) from the edge of the pastry. Remove the cut-outs from the pastry circle very carefully so it doesn't stretch or break. Place the pastry circle on top of the filling and crimp the edges of each layer of pastry together to seal the pie.
4. Whisk the egg yolk and the water together in a small bowl and brush the mixture across the top of the pie. If you want, you can add a few of the stars you cut out as decoration. Simply brush a bit of water on the underside of each star and press lightly so it sticks to the top layer of pastry. Coat the stars with the egg mixture as well. Sprinkle the pie with the cane sugar.
5. Place the pie on a baking sheet and bake in the centre of the oven for 20 minutes. Turn down the heat to 350°F (175°C) and bake until the crust has turned golden and the juices begin to bubble up through the top crust, 35–45 minutes. Remove the pie from the oven and let it rest on a cooling rack for at least 1 hour before serving.
6. The pie will keep, covered, in the refrigerator for 7–10 days.

Apple Cheddar Rosemary Pie

MAKES 1 (9-INCH/23 CM) DOUBLE-CRUST PIE

Apples are my favourite fruit, and when it comes time to harvest our orchard, this pie goes into daily rotation. The cheddar crust brings it to a whole new level! And the addition of fragrant fresh rosemary makes this pie sweet, savoury, and amazingly delicious.

1 recipe Flaky Pie Crust, cheddar variation (page 104)
6–7 medium-sized tart apples, such as Granny Smith or Honeycrisp, peeled and chopped into ½-inch (1.25 cm) pieces
¾ cup (180 mL) packed dark brown sugar
½ cup (125 mL) granulated sugar
2 Tbsp (30 mL) finely chopped fresh rosemary leaves
1 Tbsp (15 mL) grated lemon zest
2 Tbsp (30 mL) lemon juice
2 Tbsp (30 mL) all-purpose or rice flour
½ tsp (2.5 mL) ground nutmeg
1 large egg yolk
1 Tbsp (15 mL) water

1. Preheat the oven to 400°F (200°C).
2. Line a 9-inch (23 cm) pie plate with one half of the pastry.
3. Toss the apples, both sugars, rosemary, lemon zest, and lemon juice in a large mixing bowl. Add the flour and nutmeg and toss again to coat thoroughly. Let sit for 5 minutes and then toss again.
4. Add the apple mixture to the pie crust. Lightly brush the edges of the bottom crust with water, and then place the top layer of pastry over the apples. Crimp the edges of the pastry together as desired and cut four or five evenly sized slits in the top layer of pastry. Whisk together the egg yolk and the water and brush the mixture across the top of the pie.
5. Place the pie on a baking sheet and bake on the centre rack of the oven for 20 minutes. Turn the oven down to 375°F (190°C) and continue to bake until the top is golden brown and the juices are bubbling up, 30–35 minutes. Remove the pie from the oven and let cool on a baking rack for at least 30–45 minutes before serving.
6. The pie will keep, covered, in the refrigerator for 7–10 days.

NOTE: To enjoy this pie all year round, you can mix the filling ingredients in a large resealable freezer-safe bag and store them in the freezer for up to 1 year. To make the pie, simply thaw the filling before adding it to your pie crust and bake as instructed above.

Spiced Plum Tarte Tatin

MAKES 1 (9-INCH/23 CM) TARTE TATIN

This classic French dish is traditionally made with apples, but it is also the perfect way to use up the glut of plums produced here on the West Coast islands at the end of every summer. The homemade spice mix and red wine are the perfect accompaniment to the deep, tart flavours of the fruit. If you don't have red plums, this will also work with the black, yellow, Italian, or even wild varieties. (This recipe uses store-bought pastry.)

1 whole clove
1 green cardamom pod
1 whole allspice
1 star anise
1 tsp (5 mL) ground cinnamon
½ tsp (2.5 mL) fine sea salt
¼ cup (60 mL) packed brown sugar
3 Tbsp (45 mL) unsalted butter
1 vanilla bean, sliced lengthwise
1 Tbsp (15 mL) red wine
4–5 red plums, stones removed, cut into 12 even slices
1 (12- × 12-inch/30 × 30 cm) sheet store-bought puff pastry, thawed but chilled

1 Place the clove, cardamom pod, allspice, star anise, cinnamon, and sea salt in a spice or coffee grinder (see page 65). Grind until the mixture is very fine. Set aside.
2 Cut a 12-inch (30 cm) circle from the puff pastry, cover it with plastic wrap or a damp but not wet tea towel, and place it in the refrigerator to keep cold until needed.
3 Preheat the oven to 425°F (220°C).
4 In a 9-inch (23 cm) cast iron skillet over medium heat, place the sugar and butter. Cook, stirring occasionally, until the sugar has fully dissolved and starts to bubble. Scrape the seeds out of the vanilla bean pod with the tip of a knife and add them, along with the red wine and 1 tsp (5 mL) of the spice mixture, to the skillet. Continue to cook, stirring to prevent burning, until the mixture thickly coats the back of a spoon, about 2 minutes.
5 Remove the skillet from the heat and arrange the plums as desired on top of the sugar mixture, being sure to cover most of the pan. Remove the pastry from the refrigerator and place it on top of the plums, tucking the sides carefully down along the inside walls of the skillet.
6 Bake on the centre rack of the oven until the pastry is golden brown, 25–30 minutes. Remove the pan from the oven and let sit for 5 minutes. After 5 minutes, put on your oven gloves and carefully but quickly invert the tart onto a serving platter.
7 Serve warm with Vanilla Bean Ice Cream (page 143), Roasted Chestnut Ice Cream (page 147), or whipped cream.
8 The tarte Tatin will keep, covered, in the refrigerator for 7–10 days.

Raspberry Meringue Pie

MAKES 1 (9-INCH/23 CM) PIE

This pie is a marriage of Aurelia's famous raspberry cream pie and my love of meringue. Make it in the spring with juicy ripe local raspberries or in late summer with the blackberries that abound on the islands. Frozen berries work well too! If you have a kitchen torch, it's easy to toast the meringue tips to a deep golden brown, but if not, the oven will work equally well.

1⅓ cups (330 mL) chocolate cookie crumbs
½ tsp (2.5 mL) fine sea salt
⅓ cup (80 mL) melted unsalted butter
3 cups (750 mL) full-fat sour cream, room temperature
⅓ cup (80 mL) granulated sugar
2 tsp (10 mL) vanilla extract
3 cups (750 mL) fresh raspberries
3 egg whites, room temperature
¼ tsp (1.25 mL) cream of tartar
¼ cup (60 mL) superfine (berry) sugar

1 Preheat the oven to 325°F (165°C).
2 In a medium bowl, mix together the chocolate cookie crumbs, salt, and melted butter. Place them in a 9-inch (23 cm) pie plate. Using your hands or a small glass, press down on the mixture and up the sides of the plate to form an even crust of about ¼-inch (0.5 cm) thickness. Set aside.
3 In a large bowl, whisk together the sour cream, sugar, and vanilla until evenly combined. Fold in the raspberries and then pour the mixture into the prepared pie crust. Bake in the centre of the oven for 45–50 minutes. Remove from the oven when the centre is just slightly jiggly. It will set as it cools. Place the pie on a cooling rack to cool at room temperature for 30 minutes and then place in the refrigerator, uncovered, to set for at least 3 hours or preferably overnight.
4 Make the meringue just before you're ready to serve. In a clean glass bowl, whisk the egg whites until frothy. Add the cream of tartar and whisk for another minute. Add the superfine sugar 1 Tbsp (15 mL) at a time until it's fully incorporated and stiff peaks form. Spread or pipe the meringue onto the pie and use a kitchen blowtorch to brown it. Alternatively, you can place the pie in the middle of the oven under a broiler for a couple of minutes, but keep an eye on it at all times as meringue can burn quickly.
5 The pie will keep, covered, in the refrigerator for up to 3 days.

Spiced Chai Napoleons

MAKES 6 NAPOLEONS

The warming, homemade chai spice gives a surprising twist to the filling of this classic French dessert. These Napoleons are made with store-bought puff pastry and can be made in advance and stored in an airtight container in the refrigerator for up to 3 days before serving.

CUSTARD

2 cups (500 mL) whole milk
½ tsp (2.5 mL) ground cinnamon
½ tsp (2.5 mL) ground ginger
½ tsp (2.5 mL) ground cardamom
⅛ tsp (0.8 mL) ground nutmeg
⅛ tsp (0.8 mL) ground cloves
⅛ tsp (0.8 mL) ground black pepper
6 egg yolks, room temperature
⅔ cup (160 mL) granulated sugar
¼ cup (60 mL) cornstarch
1 Tbsp (15 mL) unsalted butter, cold

PASTRY

1 (1 lb/450 g) package frozen puff pastry dough, thawed but chilled

GLAZE

3 cups (750 mL) icing sugar
¼ cup (60 mL) whole milk, divided
2 tsp (10 mL) strong brewed tea, cold
1 tsp (5 mL) vanilla extract
¼ cup (60 mL) Dutch processed cocoa powder
½ cup (125 mL) whipping cream
2 Tbsp (30 mL) icing sugar

CUSTARD

1 Place the milk and the spices in a medium saucepan over medium-high heat. Bring the mixture to a boil, whisking occasionally, then immediately turn off the heat and set aside to infuse for 15 minutes. Strain through a fine mesh sieve into a measuring glass or other heatproof pouring vessel.

2 Using a stand mixer fitted with a paddle attachment (or a mixing bowl and a handheld electric mixer), whisk the egg yolks, sugar, and cornstarch on high speed until light and fluffy, 3–4 minutes.

3 Turn the speed down to medium and, with the mixer running, slowly pour in ¼ cup (60 mL) of the warm milk mixture. Whisk for 30 seconds to allow the eggs to warm. Add the remaining warm milk mixture slowly and whisk for a few seconds more to incorporate. Pour the mixture through a clean strainer back into the saucepan you used for warming the milk and cook over medium-high heat, whisking constantly, until thickened and slowly boiling. Remove from the heat and stir in the butter until melted. Let cool until just warm to the touch, about 30 minutes.

4 Cover the custard with plastic wrap, lightly pressing the plastic against the surface to prevent a skin from forming, and cool in the refrigerator for at least 2 hours, or preferably overnight. >

PASTRY

1 Preheat the oven to 400°F (200°C). Line a baking sheet with parchment paper.

2 Using a sharp knife or a pizza cutter, cut the pastry into 18 (2- × 4-inch/5 × 10 cm) rectangles. Place the rectangles on the prepared baking sheet, evenly spaced and at least ½ inch (1.25 cm) apart. Prick each one four or five times with a fork. Place a sheet of parchment and another baking sheet on top of the pastry to weight it down and then bake for 20 minutes.

3 Remove the sheets from the oven and remove the top baking sheet and parchment paper. Return the pan to the oven until golden brown, 7–8 minutes. Remove the pastry from the oven, let it cool for 20–25 minutes on the baking sheet, and then carefully place each slice on a pastry rack to cool completely.

GLAZE

1 Place the 3 cups (750 mL) of icing sugar in a large bowl and pour in 3 Tbsp (45 mL) of the milk, the cold tea, and the vanilla. Whisk briskly to create a spreadable but not watery icing.

2 Separate out ⅓ cup (80 mL) of the glaze to a different bowl and add the cocoa powder and the remaining 1 Tbsp (15 mL) of milk. Whisk together until smooth. Place the cocoa icing in a piping bag fitted with a fine-point tip, or in a freezer bag with a small hole cut from a corner.

ASSEMBLY

1 Lay 6 of the pastry rectangles on a cooling rack placed over a baking sheet. Using an offset spatula, spread the vanilla icing evenly across each rectangle and then pipe stripes of cocoa icing onto each one. Using a skewer or knife, drag the tip across the cocoa stripes in opposing perpendicular lines to form the classic Napoleon chevron pattern. Set aside to set.

2 Meanwhile, using a stand mixer fitted with a whisk attachment (or a large mixing bowl and a handheld electric mixer), whisk the cream with the 2 Tbsp (30 mL) icing sugar until medium peaks appear. Add the chilled pastry custard and whisk until completely smooth. Place this cream filling in a piping bag fitted with a 1-inch (2.5 cm) round tip.

3 Place 6 pieces of pastry on a plate or serving tray and pipe two 1-inch (2.5 cm) lines of cream down the length of each one. Top with another pastry sheet and repeat. Top the second layer of cream with a glazed pastry slice and serve.

4 These are best eaten the day they're made, but they will keep in an airtight container in the refrigerator for up to 3 days.

Five-Spice Cherry Hand Pies

MAKES 10–12 HAND PIES

Aurelia gave me this recipe and taught me that making your own 5-spice blend from whole spices leads to the tastiest results! Of course, you can also use pre-ground spices for an easy flavour boost—just make sure they're fresh. These hand pies are perfect for packing into lunches or as an easy grab-and-go breakfast item.

PASTRY

3 cups (750 mL) all-purpose flour
1½ tsp (7.5 mL) granulated sugar
½ tsp (2.5 mL) fine sea salt
1 cup (250 mL) unsalted butter, grated with a large box grater and kept in the freezer until needed
1 large egg, beaten
⅓ cup (80 mL) ice-cold water
1 Tbsp (15 mL) white vinegar
2 egg yolks
2 Tbsp (30 mL) water

FILLING

3 large whole star anise
1 (3-inch/7.5 cm) cinnamon stick, halved
2 Tbsp (30 mL) fennel seeds
1 Tbsp (15 mL) Sichuan peppercorns
1 tsp (5 mL) whole cloves
2 tsp (10 mL) ground ginger
1½ lb (680 g) fresh or frozen sweet cherries (Bing or Rainier work well), pitted
⅔ cup (160 mL) granulated sugar
1 Tbsp (15 mL) freshly squeezed orange juice
¼ cup (60 mL) cornstarch
¼ cup (60 mL) water
1 cup (250 mL) icing sugar
2 Tbsp (30 mL) freshly squeezed orange juice
1 tsp (5 mL) grated orange zest

PASTRY

1 Using a food processor fitted with a steel blade (or a large mixing bowl and a pastry cutter), combine the flour, sugar, salt, and butter. Pulse until only pea-sized butter chunks remain. In a small bowl, whisk together the egg, water, and vinegar. Add this to the flour mixture and pulse until the dough starts to come together.

2 Turn the dough out onto a lightly floured work surface and bring it together with your hands. Form the dough into a disc and wrap tightly in plastic or beeswax wrap. Place in the refrigerator for at least 1 hour or up to overnight.

FILLING

1 In a medium skillet set over medium heat, place the star anise, cinnamon stick, fennel seeds, peppercorns, whole cloves, and ground ginger. Toast in the pan, stirring often, until fragrant, for no more than 2 minutes. Do not burn!

2 Remove the spices from the heat and transfer them to a spice or coffee grinder (see page 65). Blend to a fine powder. Transfer the 5-spice mixture to a jar or airtight container.

3 In a medium saucepan, combine the cherries, sugar, orange juice, and 2 tsp (10 mL) of the 5-spice mixture. Stirring often, cook over medium heat until the cherries break down, 10–15 minutes. In a small glass, mix the cornstarch into the water to make a slurry. Mix the slurry into the cherries and cook until the mixture begins to thicken, about 2 minutes. Remove from the heat and let cool.

ASSEMBLY

1 Preheat the oven to 400°F (200°C). Line a baking tray with parchment paper.
2 In a small bowl, whisk the 2 egg yolks and 2 Tbsp (30 mL) of water together. Set aside.
3 Remove the dough from the refrigerator and place on a generously floured surface. Roll out the dough to ¼-inch (0.5 cm) thick. Using a pizza cutter or a very sharp knife, cut the dough into 5-inch (12.5 cm) squares. Place 2 heaping Tbsp (40 mL) of cherry pie filling on one corner of each square, but not all the way to the edge of the pastry. Using a pastry brush, brush the edges of each square with the whisked egg yolk. Fold the dough over the filling to form each one into a triangle and press down gently on the seams. Use a fork to crimp the edges and then place the pies on the prepared baking sheet.
4 Use a fork to poke three rows of holes in the tops of the pies. Brush each pie with the egg wash and bake until golden brown, 22–25 minutes. Remove from the oven and transfer the pies on the parchment paper to a cooling rack to cool to room temperature, about 30 minutes. Place them in the refrigerator for another 15 minutes to chill.
5 Meanwhile, in a small bowl, combine the icing sugar, 2 Tbsp (30 mL) orange juice, and orange zest. Drizzle the glaze over the cooled pies and allow it to set before serving, about 5 minutes.
6 The pies will keep in an airtight container in the refrigerator for up to 1 week. They can be frozen (before glazing) for up to 3 months.

NOTE: White peppercorns will work if you can't find Sichuan.

Caramelized Peach & Herbed Ricotta Crêpes

MAKES 8–10 CRÊPES

My dear friend Aurelia was raised by French parents—one from Paris and one from Quebec—and she makes the best crêpes I have ever eaten. This is her recipe, and it marries the sweetness of ripe peaches—fresh or frozen—with the fragrant herbs of summer. Equally perfect for dessert or Sunday brunch, this decadent yet easy-to-make dish is sure to be a crowd-pleaser. Substitute seasonal pears for the peaches to enjoy this dish in the autumn.

1 cup (250 mL) all-purpose flour
1 egg, room temperature
1⅔ cups (410 mL) whole milk, room temperature, divided
1 Tbsp (15 mL) granulated sugar
1 tsp (5 mL) vanilla extract
1 cup (250 mL) ricotta cheese, room temperature
1 Tbsp (15 mL) grated lemon zest
2 tsp (10 mL) finely chopped fresh thyme
4–5 fresh, ripe peaches, washed
1 Tbsp (15 mL) brown sugar
1 tsp (5 mL) lavender buds, crushed
2 Tbsp (30 mL) honey
2 tsp (10 mL) vanilla extract
1½ tsp (7.5 mL) lemon juice
3 Tbsp (45 mL) unsalted butter, divided

1 In a medium mixing bowl, whisk the flour, egg, 1 cup (250 mL) of the milk, sugar, and vanilla extract to remove any lumps. Add the remaining milk slowly, while continuing to whisk vigorously until smooth. Allow the mixture to sit for 30 minutes at room temperature.
2 In a separate mixing bowl, use a wooden spoon to mix together the ricotta, lemon zest, and thyme. Set aside.
3 Slice the peaches into quarters, and then cut each quarter into thirds so that you have 12 slices per peach. In a mixing bowl, whisk together the brown sugar, lavender, honey, vanilla, and lemon juice. Add the sliced peaches and toss to fully coat the peaches.
4 Heat a large skillet over medium-high heat. Add 1 Tbsp (15 mL) of the butter to the hot pan, followed by the peach mixture. Cook on each side until browned and syrupy, about 2 minutes per side. Remove the pan from the heat and set it aside to keep warm.
5 Place a non-stick pan over medium heat. Add ½ tsp (2.5 mL) of the remaining butter to the pan, and let it melt and coat the bottom of the pan thoroughly. Add ¼ cup (60 mL) of the crêpe batter to the pan and immediately swirl the pan around to cover the whole bottom. Continue to do this until the batter sets and is no longer runny, about 1 minute. Using a spatula, flip the crêpe over. Cook until golden brown, about 1 minute. Remove the crêpe and place on a plate. Repeat this process with the remaining butter and batter.
6 When all the crêpes are cooked, spread 2 Tbsp (30 mL) of herbed ricotta on one side of a crêpe, add 3 or 4 peach slices, and then fold the top of the crêpe over the filling. Use a spatula to fold the crêpe again to form a triangle. Serve immediately.

Ice Creams & Custards

Blackberry Buttermilk Ice Pops *139*

Mile Zero Coffee Pops *141*

Vanilla Bean Ice Cream *143*

Fig & Apple Ice Cream *145*

Roasted Chestnut Ice Cream *147*

Sour Cherry & Ginger Ice-Cream Sandwiches *149*

Chocolate Mint Gelato *153*

Gin-Spiked Rhubarb Sorbet *155*

Strawberry Greens Panna Cotta *157*

HOMEMADE ICE CREAMS AND CUSTARDS are some of the easiest and most delicious desserts to make, and they are infinitely superior in flavour to the store-bought variety. The base recipes lend themselves well to a huge variety of infused flavours and additional ingredients, making these desserts versatile and adaptable to whatever is in season. Below are some tips and tricks to help you master the techniques quickly.

- Ice pops (Popsicles) need at least 5 hours, or preferably overnight, in the freezer to become solid.
- A good quality ice-cream maker makes churning ice creams, sorbets, and gelatos super easy.
- Freeze the barrel of your ice-cream maker at least 24 hours prior to making the ice cream.
- Ice cream takes a relatively long time, but there's very little hands-on time involved. It's best to make the custard on day 1 (this takes about 20 minutes) and let it chill overnight to churn the next day. Churning takes 20–25 minutes, followed by 3–4 hours in the freezer before the ice cream will be ready to serve, so plan your time accordingly.
- Don't skimp on the fat content of your cream. A higher-fat cream produces richer, creamier ice cream.
- To temper the eggs—that is, to incorporate them into the custard base instead of cooking scrambled eggs—be sure to add small quantities of the hot milk very slowly to the egg and sugar mixture. Patience pays off here. If the custard scrambles, you'll have to start again.
- Add any additions—compote, chocolate chips, caramel, fresh fruit, etc.—in the last minute of churning.
- Be sure to transfer your ice cream to an airtight, freezer-proof container for at least 3–4 hours before serving. It should keep this way for up to 3 months.
- When making dairy-based ice pops, it's best to churn the ice cream for 15 minutes or so to ensure that it is thick, holds fruit in suspension, and won't split during the freezing process.

Blackberry Buttermilk Ice Pops

MAKES 20–24 ICE POPS

Buttermilk is a traditional ingredient that's making a comeback in desserts today. These ice pops blend the tartness of buttermilk with the deep, savoury sweetness of sun-ripened blackberries in a perfect combination of flavours. Raspberries, tayberries, and chopped ripe summer strawberries also work really well.

1 cup (250 mL) Demerara sugar
½ tsp (2.5 mL) fine sea salt
1 cup (250 mL) water
1 Tbsp (15 mL) vanilla extract
1 cup (250 mL) ripe blackberries
2 cups (500 mL) buttermilk, cold
1 cup (250 mL) Greek yoghurt

1. Prepare your ice-cream maker the day before you plan to make this recipe.
2. Place the sugar, salt, and water in a small saucepan, give it a whisk, and bring it to a boil over medium heat. Remove from the heat immediately and whisk again until all the sugar has dissolved. Stir in the vanilla and then pour the syrup into a heatproof container to cool to room temperature. Cover and place in the refrigerator to chill for at least 2 hours.
3. Place the blackberries in a mixing bowl and, using the back of a wooden spoon, gently crush them until they begin to come apart. You don't want to pulverize them or purée them. Simply mash them slightly so they stay chunky.
4. Pour the buttermilk, Greek yoghurt, and syrup into a blender and pulse gently to combine.
5. Turn on your ice-cream maker and pour the buttermilk mixture into the barrel. Churn until the mixture begins to thicken, 4–5 minutes. Add the crushed blackberries and churn for another 10–15 seconds. Stop the machine and spoon the mixture into Popsicle moulds. Place in the freezer for a minimum of 5 hours, or preferably overnight.

Mile Zero Coffee Pops

MAKES 10 ICE POPS

These frozen treats are based on sweet, traditional Vietnamese coffee. Don't want the extra caffeine mid-afternoon? Try a good quality decaffeinated brew, like the delicious Swiss Water decaf beans from the Mile Zero Coffee Company in Victoria.

2 cups (500 mL) boiling water
½ cup (125 mL) finely ground dark espresso coffee
1 can (300 mL) condensed milk
½ tsp (2.5 mL) flaky sea salt

1. Using the boiling water, brew the coffee in a French press or pour-over filter pot. Let it get good and strong before filtering. Let the coffee cool to room temperature and then place it in the refrigerator to chill.
2. Place the chilled coffee, condensed milk, and salt in a blender and blend until combined. Pour the mixture into Popsicle moulds and freeze for 5 hours, or preferably overnight.

Vanilla Bean Ice Cream

MAKES 3 CUPS (750 ML)

The Cowichan Valley is known for its beautiful farmland and luscious local creamery—my go-to whenever I am making frozen treats! This is the base for most of the ice creams in this book, and it makes the perfect accompaniment to any of the pie recipes. If you don't have vanilla beans, you can substitute 2 tablespoons (30 mL) of pure vanilla extract, but the beans offer an earthiness that is hard to replicate.

4 egg yolks, room temperature
½ cup (125 mL) granulated sugar
1 cup (250 mL) whole milk
1 vanilla bean, split, scraped, and seeds reserved
1 cup (250 mL) whipping cream

1. Place the egg yolks and sugar in a medium saucepan and whisk vigorously until the mixture is well combined and has turned a light-yellow colour.
2. In another saucepan, heat the milk with the vanilla bean pods and seeds over medium-low heat until it just begins to simmer. Remove the pan from the heat and allow the mixture to infuse for 15 minutes. Remove the pods and transfer the remaining mixture to a pourable measuring cup.
3. Very slowly, add ¼ cup (60 mL) of the strained warm milk to the egg and sugar mixture, stirring constantly with a wooden spoon. Still stirring constantly, gradually add the remaining milk and place the pot over medium heat until a candy thermometer attached to the side of the pot shows 165°F (74°C). Do not allow it to come to a boil. As soon as the custard reaches the correct temperature, remove it from the heat. Pour the mixture into a heatproof, airtight container and store, covered, in the refrigerator overnight.
4. Prepare your ice-cream maker so it's ready to use the next day.
5. When you are ready to make the ice cream, stir the whipping cream into the chilled custard base, pour it into the ice-cream maker, and process according to your ice-cream maker's instructions. Once the ice cream has finished churning (20–25 minutes), transfer it from the machine to a large airtight container and freeze for at least 4 hours before serving.

Fig & Apple Ice Cream

MAKES 5–6 CUPS (1.25–1.5 L)

Figs and apples ripen at the same time on our farm, and I add them both to every dish I can squeeze them into. Fig leaves are ultra-tropical, a cross between pineapple and coconut, and they bring a layer of depth that can't be replicated by anything else. I like to pick handfuls of young, supple leaves, dry them in the oven, and freeze them in a large freezer bag. They will last for up to a year and can be used in infusions straight from the freezer.

COMPOTE

1 lb (450 g) fresh, very ripe figs, stems removed
3 tart apples, such as Honeycrisp or McIntosh, peeled, cored, and diced
2 Tbsp (30 mL) brown sugar
½ tsp (2.5 mL) fine sea salt
3 Tbsp (45 mL) lemon juice
2 Tbsp (30 mL) water
2 tsp (10 mL) vanilla extract

ICE CREAM

5–6 medium-small young fig leaves, each about the size of your hand
1 recipe Vanilla Bean Ice Cream, but without the vanilla bean (page 143)

COMPOTE

1 Place all the compote ingredients in a non-reactive saucepan over medium-high heat. Stirring frequently, bring to a boil and then turn down the heat to medium-low. Cook, stirring occasionally, until the fruit is well stewed and breaking apart, 20–25 minutes. Remove the compote from the heat and let it cool for 30 minutes. Transfer the ingredients into a blender or food processor fitted with a steel blade and pulse two or three times so that you get a chunky, rather than smooth, consistency.
2 Pour the compote into an airtight glass jar and store in the refrigerator until needed. It will last up to 1 week in the refrigerator.

ICE CREAM

1 Prepare your ice-cream maker the night before you want to make the ice cream.
2 Preheat the oven to 250°F (120°C).
3 When it reaches temperature, turn the oven off and place the fig leaves directly onto the oven racks. Let them dry—do not bake them—until the oven is completely cool, about 1 hour. Tear the leaves into 4–5 pieces each and set aside.
4 Make the vanilla bean ice cream, but substitute the baked fig leaves for the vanilla bean pods. During the last minute of churning, pour the compote into the machine and mix to just form swirls through the ice cream.
5 Once the ice cream has finished churning (20–25 minutes), transfer it from the machine to a large airtight container and freeze for at least 4 hours before serving.
6 The ice cream will keep for up to 3 months in the freezer.

Roasted Chestnut Ice Cream

MAKES 5 CUPS (1.25 L)

This ice cream is the epitome of decadent! It has a rich, creamy custard base that's made all the more lush with the addition of sweet roasted chestnuts. It's delicious on its own or served with Brown Butter, Apple & Rosemary Cobbler (page 91) or Chocolate Walnut Zucchini Bread (page 59). Outside of their short season, pre-roasted chestnuts are available year-round in the baking aisles of most grocery stores.

1 cup (250 mL) finely chopped roasted chestnuts (8–10 chestnuts)
1½ cups (375 mL) whole milk
1 Tbsp (15 mL) vanilla extract
½ tsp (2.5 mL) ground cloves
¼ tsp (1.25 mL) ground nutmeg
¼ tsp (1.25 mL) fine sea salt
4 egg yolks, room temperature
½ cup (125 mL) packed Demerara sugar
1 cup (250 mL) whipping cream

1. Prepare your ice-cream maker the night before you want to make the ice cream.
2. Place the chopped chestnuts in a saucepan with 1 cup (250 mL) of the milk, the vanilla, cloves, nutmeg, and salt. Bring to a simmer and cook for 10 minutes, then remove from the heat and allow to cool completely. Once cooled, place the chestnut mixture into a blender and process until perfectly smooth.
3. Place the egg yolks and sugar in a medium saucepan and whisk vigorously until the mixture turns a light yellow colour and is well combined.
4. In another saucepan, heat the remaining ½ cup (125 mL) of milk with the chestnut milk mixture over medium-low heat until it just begins to simmer, stirring occasionally. Remove the milk from the heat and allow it to cool for about 10 minutes.
5. Very slowly add ¼ cup (60 mL) of the warm milk mixture to the egg and sugar mixture, stirring constantly. Gradually add the remaining chestnut milk and then place the pot over medium heat until a candy thermometer attached to the side of the pot reads 165°F (74°C). Do not allow the mixture to come to a boil. As soon as the custard reaches the correct temperature, remove it from the heat. Pour the mixture into a heatproof, airtight container to cool. Once it's at room temperature, transfer it to the refrigerator overnight.
6. When you are ready to make the ice cream, stir the whipping cream into the chilled chestnut custard base. Pour the mixture into the ice-cream maker and process according to the ice-cream maker's instructions.
7. Once the ice cream has finished churning (20–25 minutes), transfer it to a large airtight container and freeze for at least 4 hours before serving.
8. The ice cream will keep for up to a month in the freezer.

Sour Cherry & Ginger Ice-Cream Sandwiches

MAKES 10 ICE-CREAM SANDWICHES

These simple yet delicious ice-cream sandwiches are the perfect treat on a hot summer day. The cookies can be made ahead of time and filled with ice cream when you're ready. Try making these with Vanilla Bean Ice Cream (page 143) or Fig & Apple Ice Cream (page 145)—they pair perfectly with the ginger as well.

ICE CREAM

½ lb (225 g) sour cherries, pitted and roughly chopped
¼ cup (60 mL) granulated sugar
½ cup (125 mL) water
1 recipe Vanilla Bean Ice Cream, without the vanilla bean (page 143)
2 Tbsp (30 mL) freshly grated ginger

COOKIES

¾ cup (180 mL) unsalted butter, room temperature
1 cup (250 mL) granulated sugar, divided
¼ cup (60 mL) lightly packed brown sugar
⅓ cup (80 mL) good quality molasses
1 large egg, room temperature
2¼ cups (560 mL) all-purpose flour
2 tsp (10 mL) baking soda
2 tsp (10 mL) ground ginger
1 tsp (5 mL) ground cinnamon
½ tsp (2.5 mL) ground cloves
½ tsp (2.5 mL) fine sea salt

ICE CREAM

1. In a small saucepan, place the cherries, sugar, and water. Cook over medium heat, stirring often, until the fruit completely breaks down. Remove from the heat and cool to room temperature. Transfer to an airtight container and place in the refrigerator to chill overnight.
2. Prepare your ice-cream maker so it's ready to use the next day.
3. Make the vanilla bean ice cream, but substitute the ginger for the vanilla bean.
4. Once the ice cream has finished churning (20–25 minutes), add the cherry compote and mix just enough to form swirls through the ice cream.
5. Transfer the ice cream to a large airtight container and freeze for at least 4 hours before serving.
6. The ice cream will keep for up to 3 months in the freezer.

>

COOKIES

1 Preheat the oven to 350°F (175°C). Line two baking sheets with parchment paper.
2 Using a stand mixer fitted with a paddle attachment (or a large mixing bowl with a handheld electric mixer), beat the butter, ¾ cup (180 mL) of the granulated sugar, and the brown sugar on high speed until light and fluffy, about 2 minutes. Add the molasses and egg and beat again until well combined. Add the flour, baking soda, ginger, cinnamon, cloves, and salt, and beat on low speed until the mixture just comes together.
3 Place the remaining granulated sugar in a shallow dish. Using a small ice-cream scoop, scoop the dough into 1½-inch (3.75 cm) balls and roll them in the sugar before placing them on the baking sheet, 2–3 inches (5–7.5 cm) apart. These cookies will spread—you want them to—so pop them in the oven when they're at room temperature to allow the butter to relax quickly. Bake one baking sheet at a time until the cookies have spread and their surface looks crackled, about 15 minutes. Remove the cookies from the oven and let them cool completely on the parchment paper on a wire cooling rack. They will firm up as they cool.
4 The cookies can be stored in an airtight container at room temperature for up to 1 week.

ASSEMBLY

1 Allow the ice cream to soften slightly before using. Using a medium ice-cream scoop, scoop a 2–3-inch (5–7.5 cm) portion of ice cream onto the bottom of one cookie. Place another cookie on top of the ice cream and squeeze together with just enough pressure to spread the ice cream across the cookies. Let the ice-cream sandwiches firm up for 1 hour on a baking sheet in the freezer before serving.
2 You can store the assembled ice-cream sandwiches in an airtight container in the freezer for up to 3 months.

Chocolate Mint Gelato

MAKES 5 CUPS (1.25 L)

The abundance with which mints grow across the West Coast islands makes it the perfect ingredient for a myriad of summertime recipes, including this rich chocolate gelato. Try switching it up by experimenting with the different varietals, including spearmint, pineapple mint, and chocolate mint.

2 cups (500 mL) whole milk
1 cup (250 mL) whipping cream
½ cup (125 mL) fresh mint leaves, de-stemmed, roughly chopped
½ cup (125 mL) Dutch processed cocoa
⅔ cup (160 mL) good quality dark chocolate, finely chopped
4 egg yolks
¾ cup (180 mL) granulated sugar

1. In a medium saucepan, mix together the milk, cream, and mint leaves. Cook over medium heat until small bubbles form along the edge, but do not allow the mixture to boil. Remove from the heat and let stand for 30 minutes to infuse the mint. Strain the mixture through a fine mesh sieve and then pour it back into the pot.
2. Over low heat, whisk in the cocoa and the chopped chocolate until the chocolate is melted and the mixture is smooth. Transfer the chocolate mixture to a heatproof pouring vessel such as a 4-cup (1 L) glass measuring cup. Set aside.
3. In a large mixing bowl, whisk together the egg yolks and sugar until they begin to turn light yellow and are thick and creamy. Whisking constantly, slowly add the chocolate mixture to the eggs, ¼ cup (60 mL) at a time. Return the mixture to the saucepan and warm it over medium heat, stirring constantly. When the mixture has thickened and coats the back of a spoon, remove it from the heat and let it cool to room temperature. Transfer to an airtight container and refrigerate overnight.
4. Prepare your ice-cream maker so it's ready to use the next day.
5. When you're ready to make the gelato, pour the mixture into the ice-cream maker and churn for 20–25 minutes. Transfer to an airtight container and allow to chill in the freezer for at least 4 hours before serving.
6. Gelato will keep in the freezer for up to 3 months.

Gin-Spiked Rhubarb Sorbet

MAKES 5 CUPS (1.25 L)

This one is for adults only and is one of our favourite ways to use the glut of rhubarb that we get every May across the islands. You don't have to use a flavoured alcohol—although we love the Rhubarb Gin Liqueur from Sheringham Distillery—but the double hit of rhubarb lifts this sorbet to a whole other level.

1 lb (450 g) fresh rhubarb stalks, chopped
2½ cups (625 mL) water
1½ cups (375 mL) granulated sugar
2 tsp (10 mL) grated lemon zest
½ tsp (2.5 mL) fine sea salt
2 Tbsp (30 mL) golden syrup
¼ cup (60 mL) good quality gin or rhubarb-gin-based liqueur

1 Freeze the barrel of your ice-cream machine the night before you want to make your sorbet.
2 In a medium saucepan, place the rhubarb, water, sugar, lemon zest, and salt, and cook on high until the mixture begins to boil. Turn down the heat to low and simmer, stirring occasionally, until the fruit is falling apart, about 10 minutes. Remove the mixture from the heat and let it come to room temperature. Using a blender or a food processor fitted with a steel blade, pulse the fruit mixture, golden syrup, and liqueur until it reaches a smooth consistency.
3 Transfer to an airtight container and place in the refrigerator to cool overnight.
4 When you're ready to make the sorbet, pour the rhubarb mixture into the ice-cream machine and churn for 25 minutes. The sorbet should have thickened considerably and be spoonable but not solid.
5 Transfer the sorbet from the ice-cream maker to an airtight container and freeze for at least 4 hours before serving. Let the sorbet sit at room temperature to soften.
6 It will keep in an airtight container in the freezer for up to 3 months.

Strawberry Greens Panna Cotta

SERVES 4

If you're throwing your strawberry tops into the compost, you're missing the incredible earthy, green, berry flavour they can contribute to countless desserts. Store them in a bag in the freezer until you've gathered a couple of cups' worth and then use them directly from frozen to infuse milk for ice cream or for this delicious and creamy panna cotta.

PANNA COTTA

1 pack (each 7 g) gelatin
½ cup (125 mL) water, divided
1½ cups (375 mL) whipping cream
½ cup (125 mL) whole milk
¼ cup (60 mL) granulated sugar
2 cups (500 mL) fresh or frozen strawberry tops
1 vanilla bean, split, seeds scraped and reserved

COMPOTE

½ lb (225 g) fresh strawberries, tops removed, roughly chopped, plus a few to garnish
¼ cup (60 mL) granulated sugar
3 Tbsp (45 mL) lemon juice
1 Tbsp (15 mL) grated lemon zest
1 cup (250 mL) whipped cream, to serve

PANNA COTTA

1. Empty the package of gelatin into a bowl and top with ¼ cup (60 mL) cold water and a ¼ cup (60 mL) of boiling water. Stir and let soak until softened, 5–7 minutes.
2. Meanwhile, in a medium saucepan over medium heat, warm the cream, milk, sugar, the strawberry green tops, and the vanilla bean pod (but not the seeds) and bring just to a boil, stirring gently. Remove from the heat and let sit to infuse for 10 minutes. Remove the strawberry tops with a slotted spoon and discard them.
3. Squeeze the excess water from the gelatin sheets and add them to the warmed cream. Return the pot to medium-high heat for 4–5 minutes to bring the temperature back up but do not allow to boil. As the mixture warms, whisk vigorously until it is smooth and the gelatin is completely dissolved.
4. Pour the cream into four individual ¾-cup (180 mL) heatproof serving dishes—small mason jars or wineglasses work well—and refrigerate until completely set, 2–4 hours.

COMPOTE

1. Place the chopped strawberries, sugar, lemon juice, lemon zest, and reserved vanilla bean seeds in a small, non-reactive pot. Cook over medium heat for 5 minutes or until the fruit begins to soften. Transfer the compote to a blender or food processor, or use an immersion blender, and blend until smooth. Place the compote in a glass jar and let it cool to room temperature. Place the cooled compote in the refrigerator and let chill completely. It will keep, covered, in the refrigerator for up to 2 weeks.
2. To serve, top the panna cotta with a scoop of compote and a dollop of whipped cream, and garnish with a fresh strawberry.

Preserving

Freezer Jams & Butters

Jams and butters can be used as fillings for cakes, fruit swirls in ice creams, fillings in crêpes, or simply spread on toast for a deliciously fruity sweet treat. Jams are an easy way to enjoy fruit, such as berries, cherries, peaches, and nectarines, throughout the year; butters are similar, but they use apples and pears and are usually puréed after cooking.

- To make freezer jam or butter, simply add fresh or frozen fruit and sugar in a 1-to-1 ratio with 1 Tbsp (15 mL) of lemon juice and 1 tsp (5 mL) of vanilla extract per cup (250 mL) of fruit to a small pot set over medium heat. Cook, stirring occasionally, until the fruit breaks down, 20–25 minutes, then remove the pot from the heat and allow to cool completely.
- If you're making a butter, use a food mill or food processor to purée the fruit.
- Measure the cooled jams and butters in 1-cup (250 mL) measures, transfer into airtight containers or freezer bags, and store in the freezer for up to 6 months. Jams and butters will last up to 2 weeks in a glass jar in the refrigerator once thawed.

Syrups

Syrups are similar to jams and butters but they have a higher water content and a finer texture. Drizzle them over ice creams, tarts, pancakes, or crêpes, or use them as flavour additions to basic buttercream and cream cheese frosting, to enjoy the flavours of summer whenever you choose.

- For every 1 cup (250 mL) of fresh or frozen fruit, add ¾ cup (180 mL) granulated sugar, ½ cup (125 mL) of water, and 1 Tbsp (15 mL) of fresh lemon juice to a saucepan and cook over medium heat, stirring frequently, until the fruit completely breaks down, 20–25 minutes. Remove the pot from the heat and let the fruit cool completely before placing it in a blender and pulsing until smooth. Pour the syrup through a fine mesh sieve to remove any seeds or skins, and then transfer to an airtight glass jar.
- Syrups can be stored in the refrigerator for up to 1 week or in the freezer in 1-cup (250 mL) batches in an airtight container or freezer bag for up to 6 months. Syrups will last for up to 2 weeks in a glass jar in the refrigerator once thawed.

Herbs

When it comes to preserving the flavours of fresh herbs, an ice-cube tray is your best tool. Collect herbs such as rosemary, mint, and thyme early in the morning, preferably around the time of the full moon when their oils are most prevalent and potent. Finely chop the herbs with a mezzaluna or sharp kitchen knife and measure out 1–2 Tbsp (15–30 mL) for each compartment of the ice-cube tray. This will allow you to thaw only what you need for your recipe. Top the herbs with water and freeze overnight. When the herbs are fully frozen, pop them out of the trays and place them in a freezer-safe bag until needed. The herbs will last for up to 6 months. When you're ready to use them, thaw what you need, pat dry, and use as instructed in your recipe.

Salts & Sugars

Salts and sugars can be infused with herbs and peels that have oil—flavours such as lemon, orange, lavender, rosemary, lemon thyme, and mint. These simply need to be rubbed by hand or pulsed in a food processor at a ratio of 1 Tbsp (15 mL) herb/zest to 1 cup (250 mL) salt or sugar, and then stored in an airtight container at room temperature for up to 3 months.

Freeze-Dried Berries

Freeze-dried berries can be ground into a fine powder in a food processor and then mixed into sugar to dust over cakes, top ice cream, or use in place of regular sugar in many of your favourite recipes.

ACKNOWLEDGEMENTS

The biggest round of hugs and thanks to the incredible team at TouchWood Editions: to Tori for always being willing to take a gamble on my crazy ideas; to Nara for keeping all the ducks in a row; and to Curtis for always making me look *way* cooler than I actually am. Together you're the reasons I get to do the things I love most. Gratitude!

To Aurelia, with whom everything in this life is sweeter. I thank all the stars in the sky for the day we met—your friendship means absolutely everything to me. You are the most talented baker, pastry chef, quail de-boner, baby bouncer, stylist, author, and mum I have ever met. Thank you for your help with this book, and THANK YOU for just being you!

To Diana, this book would *never* have been possible without your kindness and generosity! Thank you for letting me into the kitchen and for lending your invaluable guidance on all things baking. I loved our conversations, our lunches, and laughing over things that go sideways in the kitchen. I hope we get to bake together again soon!

To Lesley Stowe Scott, thank you for setting me on the course toward food. I could *never* have guessed, oh so many decades ago, that I would become a full-time culinary photographer and author. From teaching me about olive oils and cheese, to the intricacies of catering, to an ever growing desire to learn about French techniques, to sending me on my first food photography workshop, you have been there at every step of this journey. Thank you for your unwavering support and belief—I hope that we have many, many more meals together!

To James, William, Georgia, Charlie, Alice, and Caitlin: I know this was a hard book to deal with . . . lol! Thank you for testing, tasting, and offering feedback on every sweet treat included. You all are the reason I love to be in the kitchen every single day.

INDEX

A

almonds

  Whiskey-Spiked Tamari Bear Claws, 28–29

Apple & Aged-Cheddar Scones, 51

Apple Cheddar Rosemary Pie, 113. *See also* Spruce Tip Shortbread

Apple Rosemary Fritters, 49

apples

  Apple & Aged-Cheddar Scones, 51

  Apple Cheddar Rosemary Pie, 113

  Apple Rosemary Fritters, 49

  Brown Butter, Apple & Rosemary Cobbler, 91

  Fig & Apple Ice Cream, 145

  Sea Salted Caramel Apples, 25

B

baking

  Apple & Aged-Cheddar Scones, 51

  Apple Cheddar Rosemary Pie, 113

  Apple Rosemary Fritters, 49

  baking trays, 5, 101

  Blackberry Sponge Cake, 73–74

  Brown Butter, Apple & Rosemary Cobbler, 91

  Buffalo Milk Cheesecake with Cranberry Compote, 95–96

  Carrot Celebration Cake, 81–82

  Chocolate Walnut Zucchini Bread, 59

  Chocolate, Cherry & Lemon Thyme Bread Pudding with Red Wine Reduction, 53

  cookies, for ice cream sandwiches, 149–150

  cooling, 5

  creaming butter and sugar, 5

  Dried-Fruit Soda Bread Biscotti, 61

  Five-Spice Cherry Hand Pies, 126–127

  Flaky Pie Crust, 104–105

  Ginger, Pear & Parsnip Cake, 77–78

  Italian Plum & Thyme Crumble, 89

  pan release, 41

  Peach & Basil Pie, 107

  pies & pastries, about, 101

  position in oven for cookies, 5

  Pumpkin-Spice Tea Cake, 93

  Raspberry Meringue Pie, 119

  spacing on baking tray, 5

  Spiced Chai Napoleons, 121–122

  Stargazer Pie, 109

  Summer Berry Sheet Cake, 86–87

  Toasted Hazelnut Chocolate Brownies, 63

  Yellow Point Cranberry Cardamom Bars, 65

baking pan, preparation, 69

bars

  Toasted Hazelnut Chocolate Brownies, 63

  Yellow Point Cranberry Cardamom Bars, 65

basil

  Peach & Basil Pie, 107

blackberries

  Blackberry Buttermilk Ice Pops, 139

  Blackberry Sponge Cake, 73–74

  jam, 73

  Stargazer Pie, 109

Blackberry Buttermilk Ice Pops, 139

Blackberry Sponge Cake, 73–74

blueberries

  Stargazer Pie, 109

bread

  about, 41

  Chocolate Walnut Zucchini Bread, 59

  Chocolate, Cherry & Lemon Thyme Bread Pudding with Red Wine Reduction, 53

  Dried-Fruit Soda Bread Biscotti, 61

  rising, 41

Brown Butter, Apple & Rosemary Cobbler, 91. *See also* Roasted Chestnut Ice Cream

brownies

  Toasted Hazelnut Chocolate Brownies, 63

Buffalo Milk Cheesecake with Cranberry Compote, 95–96
butter
creaming butter and sugar, 5
frozen, grated, 101
temperature for, 5, 41
buttermilk
Carrot Celebration Cake, 81–82
Dried-Fruit Soda Bread Biscotti, 61
Masala Chai Spiced Buttermilk Doughnuts, 46–47
butters, fruit, 162

C

cakes
about, 69
Blackberry Sponge Cake, 73–74
Buffalo Milk Cheesecake with Cranberry Compote, 95–96
Carrot Celebration Cake, 81–82
Ginger, Pear & Parsnip Cake, 77–78
Pumpkin-Spice Tea Cake, 93
Summer Berry Sheet Cake, 86–87
candy. *See* truffles, under confections
caramel
Ginger, Pear & Parsnip Cake, 77, 78
Sea Salted Caramel Apples, 25
Caramelized Peach & Herbed Ricotta Crêpes, 129
cardamom
Yellow Point Cranberry Cardamom Bars, 65
Carrot Celebration Cake, 81–82
chai
Spiced Chai Napoleons, 121–122
cheese
Apple & Aged-Cheddar Scones, 51
Apple Cheddar Rosemary Pie, 113
Buffalo Milk Cheesecake with Cranberry Compote, 95–96
Caramelized Peach & Herbed Ricotta Crêpes, 129
cream cheese frosting, 81–82
Miso Cannoli with Lemony Chèvre Crème, 18–19
cherries
Five-Spice Cherry Hand Pies, 126–127
chestnuts
Roasted Chestnut Ice Cream, 147
chèvre
Miso Cannoli with Lemony Chèvre Crème, 18–19
chocolate
Chocolate Mint Gelato, 153
Chocolate Walnut Zucchini Bread, 59
Chocolate, Cherry & Lemon Thyme Bread Pudding with Red Wine Reduction, 53
Dark Chocolate Spruce (truffle), 34
melting, 6
Milk Chocolate Mint (truffle), 35
Swirled-Chocolate Lemon Balm (truffle), 37
tempering, 6
Toasted Hazelnut Chocolate Brownies, 63
Whiskey-Spiked Tamari Bear Claws, 28–29
White Chocolate Rose (truffle), 36
Chocolate Mint Gelato, 153
Chocolate Walnut Zucchini Bread, 59. *See also* Roasted Chestnut Ice Cream
Chocolate, Cherry & Lemon Thyme Bread Pudding with Red Wine Reduction, 53. *See also* Spruce Tip Shortbread
cinnamon glaze
Pumpkin-Spice Tea Cake, 93
cobblers
about, 69
Brown Butter, Apple & Rosemary Cobbler, 91
fruit ingredients, 69
resting, 69
cocoa
Milk Chocolate Mint (truffle), 35
compotes
Cranberry Compote, 95, 96
confections
Dark Chocolate Spruce (truffle), 34
Herb-Scented Marshmallows, 22–23
Milk Chocolate Mint (truffle), 35
Miso Cannoli with Lemony Chèvre Crème, 18–19
Sea Salted Caramel Apples, 25
Swirled-Chocolate Lemon Balm (truffle), 37
Whiskey-Spiked Tamari Bear Claws, 28–29
White Chocolate Rose (truffle), 36
cookies
baking tips for, 5–6
cooling, 5
for ice cream sandwiches, 149–150
position in oven for baking, 5
Sesame-Laced Miso Biscuits, 15
spacing of on baking tray, 5
crackers
Dried-Fruit Soda Bread Biscotti, 61

cranberries
Buffalo Milk Cheesecake with Cranberry Compote, 95–96
Yellow Point Cranberry Cardamom Bars, 65
Cranberry Compote, 95, 96
crêpes
Caramelized Peach & Herbed Ricotta Crêpes, 129
crumbles
about, 69
fruit ingredients, 69
Italian Plum & Thyme Crumble, 89
resting, 69
custards
about, 135
eggs in, 135

D
deep frying, 41
doughnuts
Masala Chai Spiced Buttermilk Doughnuts, 46–47
Dried-Fruit Soda Bread Biscotti, 61

E
eggs
in custards, 135
temperature for, 5, 41, 69

F
Fig & Apple Ice Cream, 145. *See also* Sour Cherry & Ginger Ice-Cream Sandwiches
figs
Fig & Apple Ice Cream, 145
Five-Spice Cherry Hand Pies, 126–127
Flaky Pie Crust, 104–105
flavour, experimenting with, 1
freeze dried berries, 37, 86, 163
fritters
Apple Rosemary Fritters, 49
frosting
cream cheese frosting, 81–82
for Toasted Hazelnut Chocolate Brownies, 63
fruit, dried
chopping, 69
Dried-Fruit Soda Bread Biscotti, 61

G
gelato
Chocolate Mint Gelato, 153
Gin-Spiked Rhubarb Sorbet, 155
ginger
Ginger, Pear & Parsnip Cake, 77–78
Ginger, Pear & Parsnip Cake, 77–78
glazes
cinnamon glaze, 93
for Spiced Chai Napoleons, 121, 122
spruce tip syrup glaze, 11, 12

H
haskap berries
Stargazer Pie, 109
Herb-Scented Marshmallows, 22–23
herbs, preserving, 163

I
ice cream
about, 135
adding ingredients to, 135
Blackberry Buttermilk Ice Pops, 139
Chocolate Mint Gelato, 153
churning time for, 135
cookies for ice cream sandwiches, 149–150
fat content for, 135
Fig & Apple Ice Cream, 145
freezing time for, 135
Gin-Spiked Rhubarb Sorbet, 155
ice cream makers, 135
Mile Zero Coffee Pops, 141
preparation time for, 135
Roasted Chestnut Ice Cream, 147
Sour Cherry & Ginger Ice-Cream Sandwiches, 149– 150
Vanilla Bean Ice Cream, 143
ice pops
Blackberry Buttermilk Ice Pops, 139
Mile Zero Coffee Pops, 141
preparation time for, 135
icing
for Summer Berry Sheet Cake, 86, 87
ingredients
substituting, 1
West Coast, 1
Italian Plum & Thyme Crumble, 89. *See also* Spruce Tip Shortbread

J
jam
blackberry, 73
freezer, 162

L
lavender
Herb-Scented Marshmallows, 22–23
lemon balm
Swirled-Chocolate Lemon Balm (truffle), 37
lemon thyme
Chocolate, Cherry & Lemon Thyme Bread Pudding with Red Wine Reduction, 53

M
marshmallows
Herb-Scented Marshmallows, 22–23
Masala Chai Spiced Buttermilk Doughnuts, 46–47
McClintock's Farm, 95
Mile Zero Coffee Company, 141
Mile Zero Coffee Pops, 141
Milk Chocolate Mint (truffle), 35
miso
Miso Cannoli with Lemony Chèvre Crème, 18–19
Sesame-Laced Miso Biscuits, 15
Miso Cannoli with Lemony Chèvre Crème, 18–19

N
nuts
Chocolate Walnut Zucchini Bread, 59
Roasted Chestnut Ice Cream, 147
Toasted Hazelnut Chocolate Brownies, 63
Whiskey-Spiked Tamari Bear Claws, 28–29

P
pan release, 41, 69
panna cotta
Strawberry Greens Panna Cotta, 157
parsnips
Ginger, Pear & Parsnip Cake, 77–78
pastries
about, 101
Spiced Chai Napoleons, 121–122
pastry
resting, 101
sealing, 101
Spiced Plum Tarte Tatin, 115
venting, 101
Peach & Basil Pie, 107
peaches
Caramelized Peach & Herbed Ricotta Crêpes, 129
Peach & Basil Pie, 107
pears
Ginger, Pear & Parsnip Cake, 77–78
pie crust
Flaky Pie Crust, 104–105
temperature for, 101
variations for, 104
pies
about, 101
Apple Cheddar Rosemary Pie, 113
baking fruit pies, 101
Five-Spice Cherry Hand Pies, 126–127
Flaky Pie Crust, 104–105
Peach & Basil Pie, 107
Raspberry Meringue Pie, 119
Stargazer Pie, 109
temperature for, 101
plums
Italian Plum & Thyme Crumble, 89
Spiced Plum Tarte Tatin, 115
proofing, 41
puddings
Chocolate, Cherry & Lemon Thyme Bread Pudding with Red Wine Reduction, 53
Strawberry Greens Panna Cotta, 157
puff pastry
Spiced Chai Napoleons, 121–122
Spiced Plum Tarte Tatin, 115
pumpkin
Pumpkin-Spice Tea Cake, 93
Pumpkin-Spice Tea Cake, 93

R
raspberries
freeze dried, 37, 163
Raspberry Meringue Pie, 119
Swirled-Chocolate Lemon Balm (truffle), 37
Raspberry Meringue Pie, 119
resting, for pastry, 101
rhubarb
Gin-Spiked Rhubarb Sorbet, 155
Rhubarb Gin Liqueur, 155
Rhubarb Gin Liqueur, 155
Roasted Chestnut Ice Cream, 147. *See also* Brown Butter, Apple & Rosemary Cobbler; Chocolate Walnut Zucchini Bread; Spiced Plum Tarte Tatin

rose petals
    White Chocolate Rose (truffle), 36
rosemary
    Apple Cheddar Rosemary Pie, 113
    Apple Rosemary Fritters, 49
    Herb-Scented Marshmallows, 22–23

S

salts, flavouring, 163
scones
    Apple & Aged-Cheddar Scones, 51
Sea Salted Caramel Apples, 25
sesame
    Sesame-Laced Miso Biscuits, 15
Sesame-Laced Miso Biscuits, 15
Sheringham Distillery, 155
shortbread, 11–12
sorbet
    Gin-Spiked Rhubarb Sorbet, 155
Sour Cherry & Ginger Ice-Cream Sandwiches, 149–150. *See also* Fig & Apple Ice Cream; Vanilla Bean Ice Cream
Spiced Chai Napoleons, 121–122
Spiced Plum Tarte Tatin, 115. *See also* Roasted Chestnut Ice Cream
Spruce Tip Shortbread, 11–12
Spruce Tip Syrup, 11, 12. *See also* Apple Cheddar Rosemary Pie; Chocolate, Cherry & Lemon Thyme Bread Pudding with Red Wine Reduction; Italian Plum & Thyme Crumble; Vanilla Bean Ice Cream
spruce tips
    Dark Chocolate Spruce (truffle), 34
    Spruce Tip Shortbread, 11–12
    spruce tip syrup, 11, 12
Stargazer Pie, 109
strawberries
    Strawberry Greens Panna Cotta, 157
    Summer Berry Sheet Cake, 86–87
    Swirled-Chocolate Lemon Balm (truffle), 37
Strawberry Greens Panna Cotta, 157
sugar
    creaming butter and sugar, 5
    flavouring, 163
    water and, 6
Summer Berry Sheet Cake, 86–87
Swirled-Chocolate Lemon Balm (truffle), 37
syrups, about, 162

T

tamari
    Whiskey-Spiked Tamari Bear Claws, 28–29
temperature
    for butter, 5, 41
    for cakes, 69
    for eggs, 5, 41, 69
    for pastry, 101
    for sugar, 5
tempering chocolate, 6
thermometers, 5, 41
thyme
    Italian Plum & Thyme Crumble, 89
Toasted Hazelnut Chocolate Brownies, 63
toppings
    cream cheese frosting, 81–82
truffles
    about, 31
    Dark Chocolate Spruce, 34
    Milk Chocolate Mint, 35
    Swirled-Chocolate Lemon Balm, 37
    White Chocolate Rose, 36

V

Vanilla Bean Ice Cream, 143. *See also* Sour Cherry & Ginger Ice-Cream Sandwiches; Spruce Tip Shortbread

W

walnuts
    Chocolate Walnut Zucchini Bread, 59
Whiskey-Spiked Tamari Bear Claws, 28–29
White Chocolate Rose (truffle), 36
wine
    Chocolate, Cherry & Lemon Thyme Bread Pudding with Red Wine Reduction, 53

Y

yeast, 41
Yellow Point Cranberry Cardamom Bars, 65

Z

zucchini
    Chocolate Walnut Zucchini Bread, 59